C000136980

TABLE OF CONTENTS

Escape Route

I've never really thought about telling *my* story. As I sit in the here and now, it is hard for me to fully grasp that just a few years ago I was spiraling out of control and putting everything I loved on the line. In the end, it was all for a little purple liquid swilling around the bottom of an oversized wine glass.

Before I ever thought about getting sober, I couldn't fathom what could possibly be wrong with alcohol. It played such an astronomical part of my life from before I was even born. I believe our introductions were made official in the womb.

Don't get me wrong; I don't think my mother was a party animal of any sort. I am however, told that she would enjoy the odd glass of red wine, while lugging me around inside her. I also know that I wasn't breastfed and that mum's nightly glass of red wine was one of the reasons for that.

I don't remember my mother ever getting out of control or acting outrageous when drinking. For her, it was more a tradition she followed-through with every evening, while cooking up a storm in the kitchen.

My dad on the other hand was a drinker of epic proportions. I don't know if mum knew this before they got married, but I am acutely aware of the marital problems that my parents had, right up until my dad's surprise heart attack in his sleep, some years ago. What I am even more aware of, is the fact that every single argument, aggressive fight, and violent act witnessed in our home, started with that *just one* innocent drink.

"It's been such a long day! I'm dying for a beer!" That was my dad.

He would crack open a beer the moment he got home from work, and if he wasn't working for some reason (weekends for example), he would crack open one while still wiping the sleep from his eyes. My dad was a jovial guy with many friends. Many friends who wouldn't for a moment believe that once, after a bit too much brandy, he shoved my mother to the ground with a spade to her neck and watched her plead for her life.

He was so friendly and so witty that people at the local pub would hang off his every word. They would certainly be disbelieving if you told them that on several occasions he had flung a full plate of food across the room at mum, thanks to too much whiskey. After all, that wasn't what he "wanted for supper" that night.

When my dad was sober, he was calm, funny, witty, and had a naughty look in his eye. My mom had good taste back then. Long before either of them knew about the evil disease within him. That was before the toxic effects of his chosen poison made him drunkenly stray to other women too. One of these women was my very own swimming instructor, which is the basis for many of my own relationship trust issues, if I am totally honest.

Poor mum. She was long suffering and stood firm and true to her marriage vows. That's just the kind of woman she was: true to her word regardless of how low others stooped around her.

She would dust herself off and try to ensure that the next day, when the hangover draped itself over and clung to dad, he would be comfortable, loved, and doted on. Dad was always semi apologetic the next day; giving mum extra cuddles, buying her flowers, or bossing us girls around to do extra chores, so as to take the stress off of mum. What he didn't know was that we saw through it and that is essentially why my sisters and I never got too close to him as we got older.

At first, I believed that mum stayed for us kids, especially in the early years. Being a stay-at-home mom, I realize that the concept of divorce and custody issues would have been a daunting issue for her. And mum sure did protect us. Dad wasn't averse to kicking in a bedroom door, or backhanding one of us through the face, if we dared to *look* like we were displeased with him, for any rhyme or reason. As a result, mum would take us everywhere with her.

When we were home, she would protect us like a mother duck fending off danger to her chicks. Unfortunately, this meant that mum bore the beating, the pushing, the yelling – but she took it on, for us. The concept that "the danger" was *within* our home is something that weighs heavily on my mind still, all these years later.

I loved my mum, did I mention that? She did what she thought was best, albeit not the perfect thing to do. I loved my dad too, by the way. I feel that must be said. Even after everything he did when drunk; he was my dad and I guess that's built in.

I always assumed mum would leave the moment we spread our wings and escaped the nest, but she didn't. I look back on it often and marvel. I look at photos of mum back then and I realize that she was a beaten woman in every sense of the word. Mum had lost the will to live, in her spirit over the years. And the unfairness of it all is enough to push one to violent bursts of frustration. It's undeniable that she had given up and accepted her lot in life. Her life had been mostly ruined because of a drug that her beloved couldn't escape. It's the ultimate love story, in some twisted kind of way.

As we grew older I remember asking her "Why mum? Why do you stay?" and she would say "For better or worse my dear". It's these very words and the worn look in mum's eyes that made me somewhat non-committal in my own relationships. It's ironic in a way; I turned to the very thing in my life that destroyed mum's, all because I thought mum and dad's issues were about love and commitment, when in fact they were about alcohol.

I wish I could say that my parents found the help they needed. I truly wish I could tell you that mum eventually found the man she married, buried deep within the monster that took over my dad - but she didn't. She spent a lifetime with a man who imposed pain, suffering, and heartache on her. In the final years, he imposed even more pain and suffering on her, as she watched him drink himself to an early grave.

Through years of heart attacks, gout, liver and kidney problems, mum was there. And then, just like that, one night she woke up next him, and he was gone.

He never found the salvation he needed from the personal hell alcohol had him trapped in – and neither did my mum. Soon after my dad died, mum got some bad news. As fate would have it, she had cancer and yet another epic battle awaited her. And it's this that makes me realize just how fortunate I am to have the second chance I do.

Another thing I wish I could tell you is that my 3 sisters and I had grown up to be responsible drinkers, or moderate drinkers to say the least. Unfortunately, the indoctrination to drink was there from an early age and 1 of us didn't quite escape it. I guess you can tell who that unlucky 1 was.

This is where my story begins.

THE EARLY YEARS

As a kid, I spent most of my time at my grandmother's house. This was all a little before my younger sisters were born. Gran was a brilliant lady who never looked or seemed her age. She was spry and filled with a kind of excited energy that was contagious. I was only 7 years old during my life-with-gran era, but I remember it with a type of clarity one only gets when they don't want to lose hold of a really good memory. I used to spend weeks on end at gran's house with my older sister, Jo. We were too young to fully understand at the time, but I believe this was mum's way of protecting us in the early years. I have a memory of begging gran to let us stay longer and longer, with "dad's mean to mom" as the main reason. And so, we mostly lived with gran.

Grandad was around too, but he seemed to work a lot and was rather serious. My memories of granddad are somewhat hazy. Gran on the other hand was like a fairy godmother in our lives. Everything done with gran was fun. She was all about magic and adventure and she would go to the ends of the earth to make us laugh and smile. She would often say "let's make a pot of tea! Tea is simply a hug in a cup – and we could all do with a few extra hugs".

Gran also had a brightly colored "tearful tin", which she kept on her kitchen shelf. Surprisingly, it wasn't a tin full of tears. On the contrary, it was a tin filled with the comforting magic of laughter. If we ever found ourselves in a fit of the giggles, gran would grab the tin from the shelf, rip the lid off, and make each of us direct a giggle right into it. She told us we should always trap a few laughs when times were good to counteract when times were bad. When the bad days came about, we could pull the lid off the tin and allow the trapped laughter to cheer us right up. Remembering these small things about my gran often gives me hope to press on.

The night my gran died, we had to move back home to mom and dad. Grandad wasn't up for the challenge of raising small kids and "kids belong with their parents", I heard him say. I remember climbing onto a chair to get that brightly colored tearful tin down from the shelf. I also remember clutching that tin to my chest, staring deeply into it, and being almost devastated that it didn't work. I didn't feel cheered-up. My gran, my lifeline and most favorite person in the world was gone, and a piece of me was gone with her. No tearful tin or happy memory of her was going to bring her back. And it hurt.

And so back to mum and dad we went.

Soon after moving back home and settling into life with mom and dad, my younger twin sisters were born; enter Erin & Michaela. They seem to have arrived by complete accident and even though I was just 8 at the time, I knew that they were some kind of mistake. Don't get me wrong; the twins were not and could never be an actual mistake in mum's life, but were probably a mistake given the scenario. I knew this because the day mum found out, dad had a few celebratory drinks and all mum could do was cry and cry.

There was a certain sadness about her. Even at my young age, I could sense her inner defeat. Of course she didn't want to bring another set of children into this world. She didn't want to expose more of what she loved to the remnants of her alcohol-destroyed relationship; I know that now.

Throughout mom's pregnancy the arguments continued. Mum would cry herself to sleep on the sofa and Jo and I would sneak down to the living room at night, to snuggle up with her and our unborn sisters. This was the life we knew. This was our normal. I cannot help but wonder now how different our past would look, if dad had never raised the cool glass edge of a bottle to his lips for the very first time.

The Worsening

*"He punches her in the face and she falls
against the closet door. She does not strike
back as her tired body accepts its fate. He
stumbles drunkenly on top of her and grips
her by the throat. He slurs spittle in her face,
while relaying the garbled version of reality
trapped in his drunken head. The words come
forth like searing flames of hate; a confused
and twisted tale, lacking truth, lacking love,
and seeming fake. If he could only see the
pain, that's peering through her eyes. She
drops to her knees and silently pleas for mercy
from above. If he could only see that there's
nothing left, she cannot hide. He's beat her
body senselessly, now emptiness resides
inside. Tied only to him now by a promise
made in front of God; a covenant so strong
that it took from her, her heart. Things had
always been bad, but this was the start of the
worsening."*

It's the year 1990-something and I sit in class
scrawling this on the back page of my
notebook. My eyes are puffy, my throat is sore,
and I still have a sense of crying deep within
me, even though I stopped hours ago, to go to
class. By this stage, several teachers have

shown concern for my current state, but have accepted the fact that this is how I need to be right now. The questions have stopped and I am left to my own devices. It's a welcomed small mercy for the teacher standing up front to completely overlook the fact that I am clearly not listening. I am lost inside myself and nothing is important.

Last night was one of the worst nights of my life and I haven't slept a wink. Over the years the violence and aggression I had witnessed in the home were unnerving, but nothing quite like last night had ever happened. Things seemed to be getting worse and I was all-consumed by the chaos both within and without me.

Yesterday, I had caught the bus home from school and arrived a little later than usual, due to tennis practice. Mum was in the kitchen cooking dinner and gave me a quick rundown on the "state of dad". This rundown wasn't out of the norm.

"It's probably best to keep a low profile this evening, Jen." She whispered. "Dad's been having a few beers, so go straight to your room."

I didn't want to be alone, so I decided to attempt a quick run past the living room door and into my sister's room. I have run this scenario through my head a million times. What if I just went to my room as mum asked me to? Would things have been different? Essentially, it was all of my fault.

I dragged a hoodie and a pair of jeans on and prepared my escape route. I didn't think he would even notice me if I quickly ran by. I was wrong. In fact as I am thinking about it now, I can place myself right in the very moment all over again. It's funny the moments in time that the mind catches on to and keeps vivid. I am replaying it in my mind right now.

I step into the hallway from the kitchen and try to make a beeline for the top of the passage. His head jolts up and he sees me. With drunken precision, he sways his whiskey glass in circular motions and tells me to "Come here now!"

I don't quite know what to do. I am standing frozen in the hallway and Jo whispers "just go" from one of the rooms ahead of me. I venture into the living room trying to seem as nonchalant and relaxed as possible. It stinks of stale beer and whiskey in there and I am tempted to crack open a window, but don't dare.

"Hi dad, how are you?" I ask.

"Take my shoes off", he says.

I stare at him and he repeats himself in a no-nonsense tone, but with a huge grin on his face. It's a weird grin. It's not the type that you would expect to see on a happy person's face, so I assume that it is otherwise. I obey, but am unable to hide my displeasure. As I am pulling his shoe off, he kicks the shoe up into the air and it hits me full-on in the face. He throws his head back and laughs and that's when I make my fatal error. I am angry and I show it.

At the time, I couldn't believe that my pain had caused such hilarity in his mind; which really shouldn't have been surprising at all.

I say nothing, but stalk off out of the living room without removing his other shoe. I am muttering almost silently under my breath the whole way.

Moments later, I hear mum head into the living room, to smooth over any "problems" that might have occurred while I was out of her watchful sight. I cringe, wondering what will happen next. I am now safely in Jo's room, which is housing all 4 of us girls. My two younger sisters are sitting on the floor watching the television and practicing the fine art of being vaguely oblivious. A survival tactic I had to learn at an early age too.

All of a sudden, things aren't too quiet anymore. Dad is raging on about how disrespectful I was and mum is trying to calm things down by saying she will have a word with me. Poor mum. I can hear the desperation in her voice and I instantly feel bad for putting her in this position. I could have just smiled and finished the task. I could have pretended everything was fine. I am not sure why I didn't this time.

Next, there are footsteps stomping up the hallway and dad slams the door open, almost knocking Jo off her feet.

"Here's the little bitch!" he yells.

"Dad, I am sorry!" I beg as he grips me by the ponytail and pushes me in front of everyone. I am sure to be made an example of this evening and I am ready to accept my punishment. *Dad is omnipotent in this house and is to be obeyed without question* – that would be the underlying message. I can tell that mom is about to pull a familiar move and I actively wait for it. She steps in between us and tries to calm the situation down, while loosening dad's grip from my hair. I think all will be fine, but this time it doesn't work. Mum's mother duck move had failed and that's when it happened.

That's when he beat her for the first time; in front of us that is.

That night, everything became more real. Hearing it and seeing it are two very different things. Seeing what unfolded that night, opened up an entirely darker side of life to me and I still ache inside for my younger sisters, who bore witness to this at the very young age of just 7. Dad left her lying there, slumped up against the closet, on her knees. I remember she lay down for a bit with the tears gently leaking down her cheeks. We rushed to the bathroom and got a cool wet facecloth to press to her bloodied cheek. We all sat there with her silently; silently crying.

Dad of course wasn't done. That night he smashed up the entire kitchen – every single plate, cup, side plate and bowl he could find. Sadly, mum was left to clean it up alone the next day, while we were all able to head to our escape route, which at the time was school.

CONFESSION: SELF-IMPOSED HELL

I wish I could sell the idea of my dad as some kind of monster. You probably already think he was by now. I wish I could tell you that he was a mentally unstable person who beat us daily. At least that way, we could say "well, there we go, dad was just a *bad* man", but the reality is that he wasn't. The only time we caught a glimpse of dad is this way was when he was drunk, so settling on exact feelings of who dad was a man can be hard. It's still hard for me now he is long gone.

I remember mom taking active steps to try and quell the situation. We were probably allowed to sleep over at friend's houses on the weekends more than most kids were. We even had a playroom outside of the house – a converted double garage – that had some bean bags, an old couch, the smallest old television (passed down from my gran) and some of those old cartridge style TV games inside. We spent a *lot* of time out there. We would spend a lot of time away from the house on outings with mum too. We would go on visits to the library, the museum, mom's art class friends, the beach, and the park. At home, we would spend a lot of our time tiptoeing around the house, holing up in our bed rooms, or sleeping in each other's beds because of an inner sense of insecurity. We knew mom was putting in a lot of effort to limit our exposure to dad's drinking and in some way we had an unspoken understanding between us girls, that this was something to be loved and respected about mum. As kids we cottoned on to things a lot quicker than most people think and it's something I would caution current parents to be careful of. You think the kids don't notice or are unaffected, but they do and they are.

It's safe to say that mom was being proactive in her approach to shielding and protecting us, but it wasn't the *right* thing. Mom clung so strongly to her faith, her belief system, and following through on her promises and vows that it put all of us in harm's way. For a long time I didn't understand why mum stuck around. I know I had asked her before and she had told me it was her vows that kept her, but when my dad died, I stumbled across something that made me do a double take. Of course I was fully grown and out of the house by then, but it made me reshuffle the ideas I had about my dad and my childhood in my head.

The day that my dad died was a surprise to us all. For several days leading up to my dad's death, he had been behaving rather bizarrely. For starters, he had asked me and my sisters to visit him for tea. During this visit, which we only did for fear of what saying 'no' would mean for mum, dad didn't touch a single drink, besides the tea that is. He made us sandwiches and presented a cake he had apparently bought at the local bakery. He told us that he had found God and that finally he felt like he had the strength to fight the demon within him. He told us a passionate and animated story about how he believed alcohol was the gateway for this evil that welled up in him. With tears in his eyes and a red face, he begged our forgiveness. Hugging us he choked up on his words, which were something along the lines of hoping it wasn't "too late". I remember mum looking confused and uncertain of the situation. I even remember her sniffing his tea cup when he wasn't quite looking. I suppose after many years of abuse it's hard to be trusting and who knew what might have been in that cup. In the end, I remember mum breathing out what seemed to be a breath she was holding in tightly for many years. She sat there watching us with dad, tears streaming from her eyes.

That day, we left mom and dad unsure of what to think and feel. Had dad finally found the strength to escape the hell he had found himself in with alcohol? For 2 days, dad didn't drink and continued to talk along a similar vein. On the third day after our "tea party", mum said he had dinner, poured himself a whiskey (which unnerved her) and then went to bed. In the morning, with a full glass of whiskey still next to his bed; dad was dead. Jo was the first person to get to mum the next day. Mum had discovered dad dead in his sleep and had apparently gone into a state of shock. She had stayed lying there, next to her beloved, unable to move until Jo arrived to shake her out of her trance. Dad was gone. The evil had finally taken him and poor mum never even got a chance to say goodbye to the real love of her life lost somewhere deep inside him.

Mum spent the next few weeks going about life in zombie-like state, before she started to normalize. I remember meeting up for lunch with Jo and the twins and commenting on how hard she was taking it, even after all the years of abuse. "That's the cycle of abuse" said Michaela. Even though Michaela was then studying to be a child trauma counsellor at the time, I still felt a pang of guilt remembering everything the twins had gone through.

When it finally hit mum that she was free of alcohol-infused abuse, it seemed as if a fresh wave of new life was breathed into her. She didn't go through some sort of amazing transformation, but I did notice that she smiled more, she painted more, and she didn't hold back her opinions or laughter anymore. Mum had some color, not just in her cheeks, but in her very soul. It was good to see, even considering the "cost". I couldn't help but feel at the time that *this is mom's time now.*

It was around about this time that mum decided she should move away from all the painful memories of our family home. It's strange how you can watch movies about thriving families that never want to sell the family home, because it holds so much sentimental value to them. Our family was different. When dad was gone, we wanted nothing more than to get rid of that house and so we helped mum sell up and move into something more suited to a single woman with a fresh chance at life. Her new apartment was much smaller, but had a small garden for her to enjoy and enough space for her to let her previously stifled creativity run wild.

I was assigned the task of clearing out dad's desk and bedside drawers and it was while carrying out this task that I came across a little notebook with a pen jammed into it. Inside was a letter to my mother, dated a few days before dad's death, and the pages of the journal were scrawled all over with various dates on each page. It seemed to go back years. I sat cross-legged on the floor with piles of stuff around me and delved into my dad's intimate writings. What I found was nothing short of astounding. I must admit that my dad seemed to have somewhat of a secret writing skill!

One was dated the 22nd of May 1990-something.

"I woke up today feeling as if my insides were lambasted. Yesterday's meeting was nothing short of grueling. All I wanted was to yell at everyone to shut up moaning about their inane existences and get on with it. If anyone has real problems, it's me. I have 4 beautiful girls at home and while I desperately want to show them some semblance of a normal life, I can't. Alcohol is an unforgiving and selfish master and the more I grasp at being just one day sober, the more impossible it seems to be. My insides ache. If I was sober enough to cry myself to sleep last night I would have cried buckets. If I had the courage, I would put an end to it all. I would pull the trigger. I would

take myself away from these poor souls I am destroying".

To me, the entry sounded desperate and heartfelt. I had never even considered that my dad could think or speak in this way. Reading it made him human to me. It helped me see past the monster inside him and catch a glimpse of the man stuck inside; the man mum loved. I was reading the words of a desperate man who seemed to have no escape route from hell. It was a hell that alcohol had lured him into just like the Judas Goat leads unsuspecting fellow goats to their slaughter. How did he get this way? Was it sudden? Was it gradual? I suddenly found myself wishing I had taken the time to *know* my dad...to help him.

My reading wasn't done yet. Another page was dated a few days after the night dad first beat mum in front of us. It didn't say much, but it helped to resolve a bit of the resentment I had towards him.

"I have for days been looking at a spot of blood on the t-shirt I was wearing the other night. I haven't washed the shirt. Instead I keep it folded on my bedside table as a reminder of the monster I have living inside me. With every sip I taunt the monster out, but I don't

really have a choice. The monster has cast a spell on me and she gets what she wants. To see the fear in the eyes of my girls is a bitter reminder of who I cannot be for them. To create as much destruction as I did that night and not be punished; I am either blessed or there's a special kind of hell waiting for me in the life hereafter. I am thinking about an inpatient facility, but keep changing my mind. It's that or my life. I pray for the day I will have the strength to fight back and put an end to this – before it puts an end to me".

I didn't mention the book to mum and I never read the letter he wrote to her. I simply left the book on her pillow, when I went home that evening. It's obvious that dad was attempting some sort of meetings for the problems he had with drinking. Perhaps this was why mum stayed – the promise of "one day". Perhaps she was perpetually waiting for the man she loved to return to her. I never really gave much thought to the drinking side of things until I read those journal entries. I kind of believed that dad was just a bad man and that drinking simply accelerated it.

I never really considered that alcohol was the *cause*. And perhaps that's why I went down the very same road dad did, and boy did it come as a surprise to everyone. Perhaps I was a late booze bloomer just like dad. I was never a problematic teenage drinker. In fact, I don't remember getting out of control or doing anything crazy in my teens at all. I know I supped on a drink or too before the legal age, but nothing stands out to me as anything to be particularly "ah huh" about with my drinking. There was no real red flag. It just kind of hit me after school.

Let's fast forward a bit.

OUR SOULS LOCKED EYES: SHE KNEW

Remember I mentioned that mum was diagnosed with cancer shortly after dad passed away? The sad truth is that it came for mom fairly quickly, which I have always felt was rather unfair. Short of shaking my fist at the sky and trying to get into it with the Big Man Upstairs, I have merely had to work on accepting that mum is truly gone.

If I could show you my mum in a symbol, it would be the image of a really beautiful flower. When you look at the flower, it just looks like it has regular flower parts, bits and pieces, but when you take a closer look; you see all these finer details you never knew were there. And the best part is that those finer details make that flower even more beautiful.

The sad part is that mum was just starting to allow her finer details to show up and suddenly she was taken. Mum got brain cancer, which affected her left frontal lobe. She didn't make it through the operation. The reality is that we all went into mums operation with hope. We didn't for a second think she wouldn't make it, because it all seemed like a quick in and out affair. Well, as much "quick in and out" as you can get when it comes to brain surgery. One moment she was there, smiling impishly in her hospital bed as they wheeled her away. The next moment, we were all clutching at each other desperately in the hospital waiting room, sobbing about all the things we *should* have said before she went in.

In the lead up to mum's surgery, I personally put in a lot of extra time with her. I would spend a night or two at mum's, always armed with red wine. On one of these nights, mum and I got into an unexpected conversation. I suppose I had a bit too much red wine and began asking mum questions about her staying-power with dad. Mum spent a considerable amount of time thinking about her answers before she gave them and I can remember getting quite irritable with her. I remember some resentment welling up inside me. I guess I had a deep seated resentment that mum had kept us there through it all with dad. I remember slugging back sip after sip and getting more emotionally wound-up with each one. There was in instant when I looked at mum and was really about to really give her gears, when I saw something flicker in her eye. She looked dead into me. Her soft and gentle eyes prickling with tears weren't just looking at me; she was locking eyes with my soul.

To be poetic about it, she had locked eyes with that piece of inner demon I had inherited from my dad. And as If to say "hello dear friend" to an old evil adversary dwelling inside me, she merely said while maintaining gentle yet firm eye contact, "My dear child, I think in this very instant, you understand dad more than the rest of us ever could". She quietly got up, in her night gown and slippers, and left the room. There next to her chair stood the single glass of wine I had poured her earlier, untouched, as if to italicize her point. I couldn't dismiss my mom's words. Her words would forever haunt me.

THE DEVIL'S IN THE DRINK - THE DRINK'S IN ME!

"I hate you! I fucking hate you! I wish you would die!" These words still ring in my ears as loud as the day they found themselves clawing their way out of me. For someone who very rarely swears, the words seemed to be confidently hacking at the delicate fibers that still held us together. I saw the injury they caused and I reveled in it. The tears streamed down my face unabated, which coupled with the words spewing forth, made for quite a dramatic scene. How this man eventually went onto marry is a mystery to me. In fact, it's a miracle.

I launched myself at him, scratching his face and bashing the glass out of his hand. I pushed him and screamed. It was an agonizing high-pitched sound that made the reality of the situation somewhat profound. This scene was playing out in the living room of my own home. What brought it on was an overwhelming and uncontrollable urge of rebellion, or retaliation, I felt rising inside me. It was in retaliation for "not being shown enough affection" at a party we had just attended. It was a rebuttal for the attention he gave "that other girl", and it was a punishment for wanting to leave discreetly when I started chatting in an over-friendly manner with some of the other guys.

The words flying out of my mouth and the body-shaking anger I felt inside me were based solely on unfounded accusations and only spurred on by personal insecurity and of course, a splash (or a bucket should I say) of alcohol. These accusations only came to light when I was drunk and now, looking back, I see so much of my dad in me in this very instance.

Kev stood there looking at me, encircling me in a tight hug, and trying to make sense of my hatred and inner agony. I pummeled his chest with my fists and raged for about a minute longer and then relaxed into it, breathing through my anger. He didn't raise a hand. He didn't even raise his voice. He knew my story and background and yet he quietly accepted that in this moment here and now, I had lost control of my sense of self. I was no longer there and to fight it would prove useless. Perhaps my mum had been doing the same with dad, in her own way. In that instance, as I stood quaking in his arms, I couldn't help but think of mum and dad.

I wish I could say that this type of thing was completely out of the norm; a once off perhaps

– we all get one of those at least once in our lives, right? The truth is that this particular evening was hot on the heels of a similar evening we had, just last weekend.

On that particular evening, I gripped Kev's phone out of his hand and smashed it on the ground with tears streaming down my face. We were hosting a barbecue night and I'd had a glass of wine too many. I had noticed Kev responding to a text message he got from another girl. Instead of trusting him like I did when sober, I had launched full steam head into insecure drunken behavior. The fit of rage enveloped me faster than logic could process in my mind. Before I knew it, I was yelling at him and telling our guests, between angry outbursts and sobs, a barrage of untruths about Kev and how he seeks to destroy our relationship.

It didn't end there though. It was as if something else had taken over me as I went on to say that he cheats on me and that I had evidence - both lies I might add. I remember my dad hurling garbled half-truths at my mum, on some of his most enraged drunken outbursts. Now I can only assume that *this* how he was thinking and feeling.

For many years I didn't (wouldn't) actually *say* that I was an alcoholic – I refused. I would go as far as to say that I was a binge drinker and that I had a knack for abusing alcohol. I didn't quite believe that I fit in the same category as an *alcoholic*. I didn't grow up thinking dad was an alcoholic either for that matter, which in hindsight was rather misguided.

That angry outburst, like many before and after it, was not unique. The fallout was pretty much the same every time too. Much like the many times I had overdrunk and become enraged before, I spent the following day in the fetal position in my room. In fact I spent the entire day agonizing over the complexities of my life. I kept delving into myself trying to find the reason I behaved in this manner. I didn't think it was alcohol's fault. I strongly felt that there was just something wrong with me. I spent my mind to exhaustion thinking and rethinking all those self-created complexities we taint our own lives with.

I drank water like it was the air I breathed, I barely moved from underneath a blanket, and I avoided Kev like the plague. The flashbacks of the night before visited me mercilessly and left me feeling bare and desperate. I wanted nothing more than for everything to just go back to normal. I wanted him to look at me and love me and laugh with me. I wanted things to be as they were last night when he arrived.

How did the evening go so wrong? How did I go from being excited for him to join me, to telling him that I hate him? One moment we were clinking glasses and cracking jokes. The next moment, we were neck deep in an argument that made no sense. Of course, anger was oozing out of me like an unstoppable toxic leak.

I kept seeing his wounded face and his tired expression in my mind's eye. It was different this time and I was scared. Was I finally losing him? Had I finally pushed him too far? I had done this one too many times, that's for sure. I couldn't help but worry. I was riddled with worry that our long distance relationship might not handle this type of consistent upset.

I didn't quite know how to go back and turn it all around. The tears streamed down my face throughout the day and my anxiety had reached such unmanageable levels, that I couldn't bring myself to eat or sleep. As if to pour acid on my feelings of self-loathing, I had yet again phoned in sick and received the disbelieving tone of acceptance from my boss.

"I want to live a different lifestyle. I don't want this to be my story. I am nearly 40 years old and I want to make a change".

These are the words I wrote in my journal that day, but sadly it is not the day that I made a change in my life. I guess I had the same recovery style as my dad; all talk and no action. It was only about a week until I slipped back into my binging pattern and started abusing myself and Kev again.

That's the problem with drinking, isn't it? We form a pattern. We drink to excess, we spend a few days riddled with remorse, we try to get sober or cut back, and then before we know it, we slip back into that comfort of just drinking again. For me, it was no different. I would binge moderately several days in the week and then binge full tilt over the weekend. The next week was a simple case of rinse-and-repeat. The only thing that would halt this pattern temporarily would be a night like the one described above. Something terrible or upsetting would happen and I'd be shocked into a phase of self-loathing and remorse, which would slow down the self-destructive binge pattern for a short time.

I would spend a day or two crying, I would read through inspirational stories of self-growth online, I would wander through the virtual archives of sober groups on social media, and I would consider not drinking again. You know those words "never again"? I must have uttered them a thousand times in my life to no avail! In about a week (usually by the next weekend), I would be feeling better and would jump right back into binge-drinking again, as if nothing had ever happened. The pattern is hard to break. I know that from personal experience and I know that from my dad.

BEING A DOUBLE-LIFER

I was never the kind of girl that goes out, gets blitzed and then takes a random stranger home for a bit of slap and tickle. I was always far more interested in the 'getting blitzed' part. All I really wanted was to have another drink. I always wondered what the point was in calling it a night and heading to bed - anyone's bed for that matter. I was the type of binge drinker that goes out to a party and does just that: binge drinks. I was quite reliable in that sense. I wasn't in it to pick up a man, so there was no need for other ladies to ever hold onto their husbands or boyfriends when I was around. I was in it to get drunk, to fall down, and to escape all the feelings I had rattling around inside my head and my heart. I'd then to go home, sleep it off, and start the cycle all over again.

Instead of becoming giggly, flirty and enticing men with my tipsy charm, I would guzzle shots and drinks, slur shamelessly, and move on to sporting droopy eyes and a drunken stumble. I always thought it was all in good fun, but was it really? There were also times I'd puke or get upset with someone and end the night in tears. Those who were closest to me got the *special* treatment; something I learned from my dad. This included yelling, screaming, accusations and tears.

If I did wake up with a stranger, it wasn't because anything "happened". It was simply because we both needed a place to collapse – unable to do anything of any nature. That's kind of lucky in a way, I guess. Not so lucky for my liver, my relationships along the way, or my general emotional state though. It's quite difficult explaining to a boyfriend that you slept at another man's house, but not for sex. Not many partners would believe that being in another man's bed was about drunken sleep and not about drunken sex.

It wasn't always like that though. I wasn't always out at some bar drinking up a storm and staggering around. Sometimes I could quite happily drink a bottle of wine at a barbecue and not get into an emotional brawl at all.

The problem is that one bottle would turn into two and I would spend the next day huddled under a blanket, waiting for the daylight hours to pass, so that a new wave of restless sleep could envelop me. I would be happy to get just enough rest, so that the drinking could continue just a few hours down the line. For a while there in my student years, days and nights went from one drinking session to the next. But that's normal for school leavers – that's what I would tell myself at least.

I remember feeling days and days of embarrassment and shame for some of the things that happened while drunk. I would always think back on my dad and wonder if I was destined to be like him, yet I planned no real escape. I somehow thought it would just sort itself out. You know how it goes. You think that one day you will just "grow up" and all of this will be behind you. But what if it doesn't?

Over the years that passed me by, between the age of 20 and about 32, I managed to get myself quite a reputation. I was following quickly in my father's footsteps and taking up his seat at the bar. I had big shoes to fill and I had no problem doing just that. At the local watering hole I was quite well-known as the girl that could drink like a man. I could stay up late, talk out my share of drunken ideas and opinions, and keep up with whatever drinks and shots were going around. There was a consistency to my drunkenness in those days, in that I was drunk most of the time.

I was however quite the double-lifer. I wasn't *just* the bar girl with a taste for hard liquor. There was more to me than that. I don't mean that I had any sort of life sentences playing out, but rather that I was living a double life. To my family and work colleagues, I was a controlled, polite, caring, and level-headed person. They would never believe you, if you told them I fell off a bar stool on Friday night, smashed my drink, vomited on my shoes just out of sight, and then returned to the group of strangers I was with, only to drink some more. They wouldn't believe that the last time I wrote my car off in an accident, it happened at 3am, after driving home from a party that I have literally no recollection of.

They wouldn't believe you, just like others would never believe such foul things of my dad.

Much the same, if you told my drinking pub buddies that I was a shy, caring, level-headed person, that values family and has a great deal of responsibility at work (which I did by the way, I was the manager of a large firm), they would have laughed at you. That would be a far cry from the person they had seen binge-drink herself into a state of delirium, time and again.

I never retained any of my real high school friends. Because of my tricky home life, I only ever got close to a handful of people, but when we left school, we seemed to grow apart. To be fair on them, they probably found it hard to maintain a mature friendship with me. I certainly wasn't progressing in life at a regular pace. I'd got stuck somewhere along the line. A lot of my school friends were the type that got married, had kids, and went on holidays. Alcohol was undoubtedly a part of their lives, but in the odd-glass-of-wine-here-and-there kind of way. I had no place in their lives while I knocked back drinks, delved only into shallow conversations, and insisted on pulling all-nighters at the local pub.

In a way, my toxic relationship with alcohol isolated me from true and meaningful friendships, but that didn't mean that I had to drink alone. For at least a decade, I had a handful of "pub specials" who I considered to be my friends. These friends consisted of several old lecherous men, who could be found sitting in the very same seats at the bar – day in and day out – supping back on beer, smoking cigarettes and watching the horse racing on TV. There was also a handful of much younger girls and guys who frequented dodgy bars to pass the time, do a few lines, and get "smashed". It's safe to say that these were face-value friends, who probably wouldn't recognize me in the local grocery store, but still, they were my drinking buddies and in my world, that meant they were friends.

Before I met Kevin, I thought that this was pretty normal. Having people always readily-available to enjoy a drink with, at the local pub, seemed almost lucky. I didn't understand what true friendship and connections were, but now that I am sober, I find that I crave it.

What happened next was that I met Kevin.

I met Kevin in a bar. No surprises there! A friend of ours was heading to a distant country to teach English and as it happened, we were both invited to her farewell. I use the term "friend" very loosely here, as I didn't really know the girl. If I must be honest, I had only met her the previous weekend at a local bar. We had struck up a conversation, while ordering drinks, and proceeded to consume several glasses of wine together, while musing over the ins and outs of life. After staying out far later than intended and stumbling out of the pub at the wee small hours of the morning, she did what most drunk people do and invited me to her farewell the following weekend.

She probably didn't even remember inviting me and I only went, because it was a good reason to drink. My thinking was that the country was about to lose someone great and what better reason to drink, right?! Any excuse is better than none.

I remember being quite drunk before I even arrived at the farewell, and at some point I know she asked me to accompany her to the bathroom, where she quite tactfully requested that I "keep it down". To my embarrassment, the pub owner had commented on how loud and obnoxious I had become after consuming a bottle and a half of red wine. I was a fish out of water here; a different pub to my norm.

In my head, it was all good fun and everyone was having a good time. The reality was that I had forced several shots on people I had never met before. I had also stumbled and dropped my handbag at least twice, and I distinctly remember someone saying "Have another one, darling" in a sarcastic tone. I have a snippet of a memory of the others laughing quietly at that particular comment. I can only assume that I had made myself the free entertainment for the evening.

I look back on that night and cringe. The only good thing that came of it was that I met Kev. Luckily, Kev wasn't sober enough to quite notice what a colossal fool I was making of myself.

I remember being strongly attracted to Kev when I met him, which is something that just didn't happen when I was in drink mode. It took about 5 minutes of talking to him to realize that he was well out of my league. It had nothing to do with money or intellect mind you, but rather everything to do with strength of character, depth, and honesty. I couldn't match him on those, but I could certainly match him on drinking and so, for the next few times I saw him, I made it my mission to get him so drunk that he wouldn't notice I wasn't quite a catch.

It seemed to work to some degree, because Kevin and I were seeing more of each other in the weeks to follow. He wasn't quite over his ex-girlfriend, which should have been a red flag. For some reason, I believed that alcohol would bring us together and that nothing else would matter. Perhaps that's because I had used alcohol to escape my feelings for so long, that I didn't compute the fact that a man still hung up on his ex-girlfriend should be no-go territory, at least for a while. At the time, I believe that my thought-process was too marinated or "waterlogged" in alcohol to quite soak in the meaning behind it all. And so I continued to party the nights and weekends away with dear Kevin.

Kevin was great. He seemed to have a penchant for drinking just like I did and I reveled in that. Many a Wednesday night would be spent enjoying happy hour, which we stretched out from 6pm to 3am, followed by a 30 minute groping session in the parking lot. On several occasions I got him to come home with me, only for him to pass out and for me to soon follow suit. When anything physical did happen, I don't believe it was very successful, or at least I don't really remember it. Looking back, it's not a great way to build romantic memories.

I didn't quite realize what Kevin was doing back then. He was using alcohol as a distraction from the pain he was suffering with his recent break up. I had confused Kevin for a serious binge drinker like me. And one day when I realized that he was merely a regular moderate drinker in a temporary disguise, I became scared that he might see the real me. I became scared that he might look into my eyes and see the parts of me that are my dad. Needless to say, even that information and fear didn't stop me from my regular drinking sessions, or trying to drag Kev along on them. In some twisted crevice of my mind, I stored a strange belief that as long as we were drinking together, everything would be just fine.

It was the year 2000-and-something and Kevin was at the bar, very obviously not his usual drinking self. He turned down shots, he dank his beer slowly, and he didn't have that normal drive to get blitzed as he usually did. I decided I would need to turn up the charm; you know, really come on strong. I wanted to take the party up a notch and get things going. I dangled a row of 3-tequila-shots-each in front of him like a bunch of tantalizing carrots before a donkey. He looked up at me half amused, half sad, but then out tumbled the dreaded words, the type of words I had been half worried about.

"Jen, we can't keep doing this. I was upset about my ex and drinking my way through it when we met, but this can't carry on. I like a good drinking session, but we have been going overboard. This isn't fun anymore – it's merely damaging."

I was flabbergasted. And to be honest, I felt quite awkward being flabbergasted with 6 tequila shots sitting in front of me. Whatever did he mean? The drinking cannot go on? And more importantly, what will happen to these tequilas?! These thoughts were all but pickling my mind as he spoke.

I shot back at him a little over-defensively; "I thought you liked me, I thought we had something good happening here. I thought we were having fun! And now I am just not good enough?!"

Kevin wasn't slow to reply – it's something I have come to love about him, because it means he knows what he wants and has no problem saying it. The words hit me like a ton of bricks though.

"I do like you, but this lifestyle isn't entirely for me. The parties are fun, Jen, but they're weighing me down. This isn't drinking for fun. This is drinking for end-game. It isn't right". He paused briefly and took in my expression. "I should probably also tell you that I have been offered an open-ended work contract. I am worried that a relationship of *this nature* just won't survive a long distance relationship".

The silence hung between us for a few moments.

I remember bumbling my way through promises of all the drinking being "just a phase" and making promises to change. It's funny how desperation will make you say almost anything. I remember saying a bunch of things I would roll my eyes at nowadays.

I remember my dad doing the same thing to my mum, especially after a drinking binge. Mum would be unhappy and dad would promise great change. Dad would promise to wrap the world in a glass box for mum and now I was doing the same to Kev.

Perhaps Kev made it too easy for me. Perhaps he should have made it harder for me to get what I wanted, without seeing any evidence of real change first, but he didn't. And that night we agreed that we would slow down on drinking and give a long distance relationship a shot.

I didn't know then that telling someone you will cut back actually meant something. I wasn't fully aware that you can't just give up drinking purely for someone else. You have to find a way to give up drinking, first and foremost, for yourself. I know now that *that* is the only way you truly give up drinking.

A Decisions: Quit Drinking

Have you ever asked yourself "Am I an alcoholic?"

I would be lying if I said I *never* thought about it. While I have always been very good at pretending my past is behind me, I often considered my dad's behavior and wondered if my binge-drinking ways are just in my genes.

If anyone asked me if I thought I was an alcoholic I would have said no, but I must admit that after a number of years, suddenly the jury was out on that one. I kind of knew I was toying with the acceptance of being an alcoholic when I caught myself quizzically monitoring how others drank around me. My sisters would often be the subjects of my monitoring and because I found myself to be an excessive drinker by comparison; I came to the conclusion that they are those elusive and unnatural "just one glass" beings. It seems that my sisters' childhood experiences had the opposite effect that mine had on me. I consider them lucky.

I was toying with the idea of self-confessed alcoholism for quite some time before it eventually became something I was certain about. The decision to claim my title as alcoholic and venture into an alcohol-free life came at an awkward time.

I was deeply ensconced in a relationship with Kevin at the time. The realization that one of us *had* to quit drinking, if our relationship was to survive, came into my life as a searing hot reminder of my childhood. The feelings tore through me like a hungry angered dragon, snapping away at bits of meat left on an old carcass. As I allowed each feeling, each memory, and each thought to bore a hole into me, I knew that the person to quit had to be *me*.

It wasn't that I thought I wouldn't be able to inspire change in Kev. It wasn't that I felt I needed to prove that being sober was a happier and healthier way to live. It was mostly because I had an epiphany. And in that epiphany, I realized that what dad was doing to mom all those years back, I was now doing to Kev.

More than that, I realized that I was doing it to myself. I was allowing myself to get trapped in the very same hell that dad had lost the battle to. I remembered dad's journal entries and the way the years had spanned out through my childhood and I just *knew*. This was a demon I had to beat now, before it became too late.

I had no intention of pushing Kevin into a lifestyle change, when *I* was the one with the problem. I was the one that always took it too far. I was the one who couldn't moderate. I was the one that suddenly changed when drinking. I was the one who started all those fights. I was the one that got aggressive and violent when drunk. It was me, all me – it certainly wasn't Kev.

This epiphany hit me one morning as I lay on the floor *next* to the bed, instead of in it. I had a hangover sent straight from hell, smudged make up, and crusty tear residue pinching the skin of my cheeks. I was wearing last night's dress and the taste-and-smell of old cigarettes, stale beer and wine was literally oozing out of me.

The bruises on my arm, cuts and scrapes on my legs, and the flashbacks to the nasty antics shot back and forth between us last night, served as a stark reality check. Was *this* my life now? Was some version of mum's and dad's life now mine? Did I inherit dad's demon when he left this earth? My mind was reeling.

I was instantly aware that *this* wasn't what I wanted *and* that it was really all *my* fault that I was *here* in the first place. I had spent most of the night awake, thinking and over-thinking things in my head. I knew I had to make changes and 2 particular changes seemed obvious to action right now.

1. I had to relocate, to live with Kevin – long distance just wasn't working.

2. I had to cut booze out of my life.

I didn't come to these realizations on my own, on a whim. Oh no, definitely not. Another "episode" had transpired and I knew the only way to stop them from happening time and again, was to acquire a firm "enough is enough" approach to my life.

What transpired was another one of *those* nights. It had been a friend's wedding the previous day and we had attended with good intentions. Kev and I were living separately while trying to navigate the challenges of our long distance relationship. To be honest, I had become quite tired of traveling up and down and the unsettled lifestyle was placing unwanted pressure on our relationship. When I had arrived for this particular visit, I had approached the topic of truly committing to each other and Kev had outwardly said he wasn't sure if he was quite "ready to commit".

At this point all the ladies reading this are probably rolling their eyes and thinking that I should have run for the hills, but the relationship between Kev and I was somewhat complex. Before he said "I don't know if I want to commit", I had been saying it for months myself. I was the one who allowed this kind of confusion to creep into our relationship. And can you really blame me? In my mind's eye, adult relationships were destined to be fraught with problems. I remember my mom being subservient to my dad and I strongly remember him taking her kindness and loyalty for granted. Even after my dad's death, mum only ever spoke about the times before they were married. She spoke fondly of these times, as if the problems only hit when the confetti fell to the ground, after the wedding. I didn't want what my mum had for a life. I just didn't realize that in my attempt to have a different life to mum's, I was actually imposing that very same life on someone else; Kev. I was becoming my dad.

Prior to the night of the wedding party, Kev and I had been fighting more frequently. My current visit, which was just for 12 days, was coming to a close and we *still* hadn't really addressed the issues at play. I was feeling insecure, unwanted, and confused by my own change of feelings towards commitment and Kev's too. I had a gut feeling that going to this wedding wasn't going to end well, but I pushed that thought out of my mind. Wine would be there and that would make it okay. At least that's what I thought. I had been worried about the amount I had been drinking recently and had mentally decided that 2 glasses of wine was enough. As they say; famous last words.

After several glasses of wine and a bunch of insecurities rattling around my head - I have a vague recollection of this – I started chatting to another man at the wedding reception. I can't for the life of me remember his name or what was so alluring about him, but I do remember reveling in the jealous stares I got from Kev as I gave this man my number.

What was I thinking? Why was I giving another man my number at a wedding right in front of Kevin, as if he wasn't even there? Heaven (or hell) alone knows and what ensued was to be expected. Kev was furious to say the least. I of course, was indignant and refused to see where I was going wrong. This all happened just before the music was revved up and the dance floor came alive. I could see Kev trying to desperately save what was left of the night. He shook it off, told me we would address the matter at home, and headed to the dance floor, to make a few requests and dance the night away.

I couldn't just let sleeping dogs lie. My mind was running wild and I just couldn't let it go. How could this man, who rejected me with his non-committal approach, be left to enjoy his evening? The cheek of it, I thought! My drunken mind had taken over and all reason escaped me like a tired breath.

I ventured over to the dance floor and wobbled around a bit, much to the delight of the bride. And then I made things worse by waffling and crying on the bride's shoulder for what must have been an eternity. To this day she hasn't forgotten how I cried, badmouthed Kev, and used her as a source of comfort on HER WEDDING DAY. And neither have I. The shame still lives within me. I was *that* person.

It had apparently become quite obvious that Kev and I were having a shift in alignment that evening, so he made the decision that we should leave pronto – and that's where I start

hitting several blanks in my memory. The free
drinks at the bar certainly didn't help me – I
know that now.

I have racked my mind over the years, trying to
understand what ensued on the drive home,
but it's pretty hazy and confusing to say the
least. I know that at some point of the drive up
the unfamiliar road towards our hotel, I opened
the car door and dramatically threw myself out.
I tumbled onto a gravel side road and shredded
my dress, legs, shoulder and a bit of my face. I
looked a treat the next day, that's for sure. I
also know that when Kev tried to help me back
into the car, I had punched, kicked, screamed
and hurled all manner of profanities at him.

Other guests, who had left at the same time as
us, had seen the "accident" and stopped to
help. I am told that they were utterly astounded
at the demon that stood before them (and that
demon would be me by the way). Some of those
people were so shocked by my behavior that
night that they saw fit to delete me from their
social media profiles. It must have come as a
surprise, as no-one would ever believe such
hatred could pour out of such a petite, good-
natured *seeming* person. The problem is that
they were judging me on who they had met

when I was sober. And drunk Jen is officially someone else completely.

I assume that I slept the rest of the way home (Kev was so mad that we drove straight on past the hotel and back home). I know this because I remember waking up as we drove into Kev's driveway. The 2 hour trip had done nothing for my state of mind and I sought only to create more harm the moment I opened my eyes. Living in close proximity to his work colleagues, I can only imagine how embarrassing such a scene must have been for Kev. I know I threw a beer bottle at him and screamed a bit more – definitely loud enough for everyone in the apartments nearby to hear.

I eventually tired out, when I realized I was getting no response from Kev and in some show of protest, I slept on the floor next to the bed, so as not to suffer the mere sight or touch of him. This was very mature of me to say the least. And of course, this felt all too familiar.

These cycles sound terribly uncomfortable, but they become sort of a comfort zone, don't they? You get used to drinking, feeling buzzed and sometimes going overboard. You get so used to the cycle that you start to excuse abusive behavior to a partner, or overlook the fact that you nearly killed yourself rolling out of a moving vehicle.

You start to assign less and less guilt to hurting someone you love, because "I was drunk" seems all too convenient an excuse. As a child, looking on at this very type of behavior happening in my own home, I was traumatized. I remember longing for a different life. I remember looking at mum, hoping and praying that life would change for the better for her. Knowing this, you would think that I would avoid it at all costs in my own life when I got older, but for some reason, I had merely inherited the cycle and was continuing it. And I was readying it to be passed on to the next generation of my own family.

I had gotten so used to drinking to delirium, freaking out, sleeping it off, sobering up, wallowing in self-pity, and then repeating the cycle again; that it had become the norm. Just like it became the norm for my dad to drink himself sick, treat mum and us girls with aggression, be remorseful the next day, and then start all over again. I had done this type of night and next-day on repeat, so many times in my life. I had done this so many times to Kev.

The scary part is that this night was not the worst it had been between us. That gives me cause for cringing. There's no way around it; I am (and was) a bad drunk.

During *those* days, I almost felt that if I admitted I was a bad drunk I would be saying that something was wrong with me. I would be admitting that I was my dad, or at least very much like him. Even though my behavior when drunk was delivering a message far worse than that, I just couldn't get myself to admit the actual problem.

I was scared of labeling myself and I was terrified of saying "never again" to a drink. Now, several years into my sobriety, I can confidently say that I know that there is nothing wrong with me.

Alcohol is a chemical and a drug. It affects the brain differently in each and every person. While one person might have 2 beers and be happy and pleasant, another can have 2 beers and become highly intoxicated, outraged, and emotionally unstable. This is the nature of chemicals and the brain. And anyone who feels "less than" because they become a bad drunk, is wasting emotions on a science they will never understand. They should rather put their effort into beating the problem – avoiding it completely.

I firmly believe that some people can drink and others can't. And if you are anything like me, and just can't moderate, then you *can't*. There is no cure to this affliction. The only way out is to abstain.

Let's get back to the decision.

As I lay there on the floor, I knew that I had broken a very delicate, already partially damaged relationship between myself and Kev. I had been allowing alcohol to drive a wedge between us for so long that I didn't quite know how to backtrack and change it. I was so scared to break ties with my best liquid friend that I allowed it to break us instead. And that day as Kev lay looking down on me with the saddest expression in his eyes, I knew I had lost a part of him (and us) that I might never get back. Last night was just too much, especially when added to the plethora of drunken woes I had already unleashed on our relationship. I was terrified.

KEV, THE ENABLER

We all know that I'm the monster in this particular story, but you haven't heard the whole story yet. What you don't know is that while Kev was not the instigator of a booze-fuelled fight, he also wasn't *just* a participant. Kev was the actual *enabler*.

You see, Kevin didn't like the fights that we got into when we drank, but he would never say that out loud. Perhaps he couldn't admit that *alcohol* was causing it. Perhaps he loved me too much and didn't want to hurt me with the truth.

He wasn't opposed to a good drinking session, but never truly understood the true evils of alcohol. Kev never had a problem with alcohol like I did and he was brought up in a very clean cut, straight laced family.

Kevin was lucky enough to be able to *choose* whether to drink hard or moderately on any given occasion. I believe I never had that luxury. Drinking could only be done hard and at full tilt with me. Moderation was not an option. Kevin was unable to understand my drinking problem, because for him, drinking was something one could either do or not do in life – it was a choice and it didn't rule him. He decided. *He* was in control.

In a way, I think that Kev thought that "us" quitting would mean that he could never enjoy a drink again. Perhaps he thought the fun times would end. We didn't speak about my alcoholism nearly as much as we should have.

I think I was scared of the same thing as Kev, to be honest. I was worried that if I actually committed to "not drinking", the fun would come to an end.

Because of Kev's lack of understanding and our combined fears, he did a fine job of convincing me (and mostly himself) that it "wasn't that bad" or that my outbursts and anger only rose to the surface "sometimes" when drinking. The general idea he had in his head was that there was no need to give up drinking completely, seeing as my outbursts, angry rages, and insecurities, only rose to the surface occasionally. It was almost as if he thought this was a problem that would sort *itself* out. I got the impression he thought this was some kind of phase. I knew better though!

Kev would happily pour me a drink, just days after a colossal all-out booze-fuelled war between us, and not see the danger in it. Perhaps he was just completely unaware – I have never really asked him about it. What he didn't seem to realize was that while I had a love for alcohol, I desperately wanted to rewrite my story and he wasn't helping by telling me I didn't have a problem, when I told him that I did. I had turmoil inside me that I needed to deal with and alcohol was only stirring that turmoil up more.

It didn't help me when he had big drinking nights, when I was trying to quit. And it didn't help me that he liked to binge just as much as I did on occasion. It didn't help me that he could say no to a drink when I couldn't. But one thing I will say about Kev is that even though he had all these enabler flaws and was mostly unaware of my problem in its true sense; he was always there for me and that counts for a lot. In many ways, Kev inspired me to quit.

The Party's Over: Time to go Home

The party has to come to an end at some point. It always does, doesn't it? You don't go to a party that never ends. If you did, you would get tired, crabby, and probably look for an escape route at some point along the way. The truth is, we all need sleep, rest and repair!

That's what happened with me and alcohol. The party came to an end. I *knew* it was going to be tough, but the only way to enjoy my life was to live without alcohol. This knowledge bore down on me heavily and I honestly felt like I had no-one to help carry the load. It was like I was making the hardest decision of my life. I knew the decision *had* to be made, but I also had this overwhelming sense that it was locking me into some sort of lifelong contract. It was terrifying to think of "forever". The whole thing seemed almost impossible.

I had real fears going forward. I wondered all manner of outrageous things. I wondered if Kev would leave me because I was now deemed boring. I worried that I *was* now boring. I was terrified of social occasions and all those get-togethers we had already planned on our calendar. I felt like putting it off to a more convenient time, but I kind of knew that time would never come if I did.

A life without alcohol seemed like a tall order, but I had to do something. I had to make a change and there was no way around the harsh reality that no one else could fix this, but me - and so I took the plunge.

If I think about my very first day sober, I remember being like the new kid in the class. I was awkward about it. I didn't know where to start. I was so twisted up inside about the decision that I felt completely overwhelmed. I kept remembering what mum said to me that night in the days leading up to her passing.

"My dear child, I think in this very instant, you understand dad more than the rest of us ever could".

The memory of that was tearing me apart.

At the same time, I wasn't sure if "sobriety" meant just not drinking, or if there were things I needed to do along the way that would help me *earn* my sobriety. I didn't know if I should be counting the days, looking for a sponsor or taking medication. I basically knew nothing. All I had was a desire in my heart for things to be better and an intense ingrained fear of what that would mean for me. It was like I had awoken from a trance and suddenly I knew that I was doing everything wrong. But even though I knew that, I didn't know how to change what I was doing. It was a time filled with a whirlwind of emotions, that's for sure.

What I have learned is that there is no right or wrong way to quit booze – it's really about what works for you. Some people join AA and do the steps (unfortunately that was never for me) and others join online groups or go to rehab facilities. Some can just empty out or lock the liquor cabinet and resist, while others can't get through the day knowing that there is alcohol in the house. I have tried several times to quit drinking and I finally found a method that worked for me (and it still does), which I will share with you towards the end of this book.

The first day of my sober life was a hangover day and I must say that it wasn't pretty. I have read of people feeling so motivated and inspired by their decision to get sober that they glamorize the process. Some people post motivational quotes on their social media pages and make grand promises to their partners. I didn't do any of that. I entered my first day of sobriety in quiet contemplation and with intent.

I hauled myself up off the floor next to the bed, stomped off to the bathroom, cleaned myself up and spent the day moping, just like I would any other hangover day. I was almost scared inside that I would suddenly change my mind and regret making the decision, so I didn't say anything about it at all to Kev.

The day was accented with bouts of uncontrollable tears, spurred on by high levels of anxiety, and just general drinker's remorse. I was trying to quell flash backs of the previous night *and* my child hood in my mind. I spent a considerable amount of time sending off a tirade of desperate apology messages to our friend, the bride. Of course, the messages remained unanswered, only inspiring fresh bouts of anxiety in me. Sometimes you just need to hear someone say that "it's okay". I didn't get that. To top it all off, I ate piles of greasy food too. As far as hangover days go, it was pretty up there with the worst of them.

Kev on the other hand spent the day pensively keeping a safe distance between us and trying not to notably wince every time he saw my bruises, cuts and scrapes. For the most part, my entire being suffered complete and utter embarrassment. I was exhausted and riddled with anxiety. If you have already gone through your first day sober, perhaps yours was different, but know this; there is no ideal first day in sobriety.

Nowadays I consider my first day as some sort of rebirth. It was messy. It was ugly. It was painful. But it was the start to something truly beautiful. It was the birth of a whole new life and those days were the very start of the formative years. I must admit that the person I have become through sobriety is someone I like a whole lot more than the previous version of me.

Getting to Grips With It

Everyone has their ups and downs and that's just fine and normal, but when I decided to go alcohol-free, I found that the severity of these ups and downs was greatly exacerbated. The first few weeks were not easy and I was anything but a positive ray of sunshine.

Just a few months prior, I would have eagerly turned to a glass of wine to take the edge off after a rough day or to ease myself into a social situation. Now, I no longer had that crutch. I ached inside and out from sheer and utter frustration. It took at least 3 weeks for me to get through the physical discomforts and then what came next, was the emotional issues I had to deal with. Escapism through alcohol was no longer an option.

I remember writing myself a letter to help me remember why it was so important to get sober and stay sober.

Dear Self,

You spend your life making big romantic gestures to start things...and over time you do nothing to end them. It seems to take a life time for you to build things up and less than a moment for you to break it all down.

You fill your life with a "thing" that makes you happy, or are you simply distracting yourself

*from all the things that make you sad? I see
through you...*

*You are a soul with a heart at its best when it
truly smiles.*

*With the anticlimax of a poorly started life, it
is no wonder you feel an all-encompassing
heartache. In your life you wax and you wane.
You are ruled by an emotional force that you
cannot control. Don't try to cage or stifle what
you heart is telling you it truly desires. Your
heart will break free one day, just like your
soul. Discard the commands of the disease
wreaking havoc within you. It doesn't know
what's best for you. It seeks to destroy you just
like it did dad. Don't let it take you.*

*You like to think that things in life are
uncertain but know this; you make mistakes
and you have regrets. And while you think
they don't define you or shape your life, you
are undeniable proof that they do.*

*Today is the day that you commit to a change
that will deter you from the path of
destruction you previously chose for yourself.
Make this change in dad's name. Do it for
mum, do it for you. Do it for all the little things
in life that matter, because one day you will
look back and want memories. Right now all
you will see when you look back is alcohol and
emptiness."*

To be honest, I wrote this letter because I didn't trust myself, but I am glad that I finally found it in myself to listen to my heart, get sober, and take control of what defines me and my life.

When I think about it, I don't believe I would have had that very first sip of alcohol if someone had told me that quitting one day would be terribly hard. I don't think I would have deemed it worth it. It doesn't come as a surprise though. Alcohol is a chemical that is addictive to the human body – naturally it is a hard one to quit.

In the first week of being sober I toyed with the thoughts in my own head quite a lot. I could often be found curled up on the couch with a cup of tea, simply staring ahead, thinking. I was reorganizing what I thought I knew in my head. On one of these afternoons of languid staring ahead with a steaming cup of tea, I got to thinking about the illusionary tipsy feeling that I had become so addicted to.

In reality, being tipsy or happy drunk is the ultimate illusion. It's just not real. It lies to you. That's the conclusion that I came to.

It wasn't just sitting on the couch and staring ahead that helped me get to this conclusion. I also owe this great epiphany to experience.

When I set my mind to and alcohol-free lifestyle, something I really wanted was to keep living my life as normally as possible. I didn't want to shake things up too much or go out of my way to make my life turn into something I no longer recognized. In hindsight, this is a misconception on my part. I wanted everything to change for the better, so it logically stands to reason that I would need to change my lifestyle quite dramatically, in order to achieve that. This type of logical thinking was only something that I gained later on though.

In my quest to go about my life as per usual, I decided I would keep doing what I was doing, sans alcohol. This decision ultimately meant that a trip down to the local pub on the weekend with Kev and some mates wasn't to be avoided. For some, this is a futile exercise, so I am not recommending that you socialize in a bar or pub environment, before you are ready for it.

I remember one particular Saturday afternoon when we headed down to the pub; I decided I would try my best to be the same Jen everyone in our group had come to know and enjoy. The only change would be my mind set. I was adamant that I wouldn't drink.

At first, everything went perfectly well. We usually have everyone meet at Kev's place and then take a walk down to the pub together. The walk was jovial as usual with everyone catching up, acting silly, and generally revving up the mood. It goes without saying that everyone was salivating for their first drink and talking almost incessantly about it on the way. That was to be expected, I suppose. I couldn't really expect everyone to suddenly be on the road to drinking less, just because I had some sort of epiphany that spurred me on to a life of sobriety.

I wanted to expect that though and it was hard to push those feelings down. I wanted to shake my first at the sky and bellow up to the heavens about the unfairness of it all. Instead, I had to realize that I could be sober and want what is best for me and those around me, but I could not *impose* my sobriety on other people. I *knew* that and it made me grit my teeth irritably.

On initial arrival at the pub, all went seemingly well. I flitted straight off to the ladies' room. I was really just hiding out from the first round of drinks. Mission success!

From within the toilet cubicle, I started to feel my anxiety rise. I had been in the pub less than a minute and I was already telling myself that it wouldn't be fun without a drink and that I should just have a few to get in the mood. My resolve was flip flopping around like a fish out of water on the floor. One moment I was adamant I wouldn't drink and the next I was thinking "what the heck, it's just a few".

When I eventually gathered myself and took a few deep breaths, I started to consider my options. After all, I hadn't told anyone, but Kev about my new found sobriety yet! I contemplated heading to the bar to order myself an alcohol-free beer. This would at least trick the others into thinking I was drinking, which would take a lot of pressure off me. I decided to do just that. I had absolute faith that an alcohol-free beer would help me avoid questions, pressure, and the urge to drink that was currently niggling at me.

With that, I grabbed my bag and headed out of the bathroom. As I emerged, Kev's eyes were fixed on me. He didn't have to say anything; his eyes delivered the "what's happening with you?" message rather clearly. I gestured to show him that I was headed for the bar and all but scampered in that direction. With a bit of privacy from the watchful eyes and ears of the group, I leaned on the bar, standing on tiptoes and scrutinized the drinks snugly packed into fridges and shelves. I remember thinking that the barman looked far too young to be serving alcohol!

"Do you have any alcohol-free beer?" I asked softly.

"What?" he replied a tad louder than I was comfortable with, "What do you mean by alcohol-free beer?"

I knew it was the end of the game for me. If the barman doesn't know what an alcohol-free beer is, you can be certain that the pub or restaurant doesn't serve it. I settled for a club soda and a slice of lemon and headed back to the table somewhat disgruntled.

I had a feeling of dread creeping up within me as I made my way back to Kev. I wish I knew then, what I know now.

I had this image of someone ultra-cool and relaxed, not drinking, and also not giving a damn what anyone else thought about it. I wish I could have been that person, but at that stage, I just wasn't. Being that way is the dream, but we all know that it doesn't work like that for a lot of us. For a lot of us, these occasions spell dread.

We *do* want to drink. We *do* care what other people think and say. And their reactions *do* affect us. We do get an overwhelming fear of missing out when people are getting raucous around us and in comparison; we are sober as a nun.

Don't let this put you off getting sober though, because I can confidently tell you that this all changes somewhere along the way. Nowadays I don't feel like drinking when people drink around me and their reactions to my sobriety are more amusing than they are hurtful or frustrating.

Let's fast-forward about 30 to 40 minutes into the occasion. My sparkling water and lemon drink, was almost immediately called to the group's attention. I have come to realize over the years that drinkers are like finely tuned sniffer dogs. They can immediately recognize an alcohol-free drink that is in their immediate surroundings. It's almost as if the mere smell and presence sends them into high alert! I was outed with a great resounding Jen isn't drinking today/tonight. The truth was out!

It doesn't take long for people to start applying group pressure. It wasn't very long at all before I was lugging a vaguely annoyed attitude around with me. What annoyed me most was that Kev was joining in on the "Have just one" comments. While I wanted to glare daggers at him, I didn't dare, in case someone caught it and put me down to a "poor sport". At some point I managed to force myself to behave in a good-natured way, but in reality, I just wanted to scream, cry, and run away.

It had been a glorious week of no fighting between Kev and I (surprise surprise). While I was going to bed earlier and lacked general Jen-like spark, I felt a sense of accomplishment starting to take hold within me. I felt as if I was actually getting somewhere, for the first time in my life. I wish I could have communicated this to the group, when I was feeling it. I think it would have made a huge difference as these people were genuine friends; friends who would have cared enough to make it easier on me. We have spoken about it since then and it has made a considerable difference to the way we connect. It took a really long time for me to get to that point though.

I wish I had been able to tell the group just how much it would mean to me if I could spend time with them, *without* drinking. I needed them to understand that this wasn't just a spur of the moment thing that I was trying out. I had no idea how to say the things that I felt in my heart. I wished they knew just how important this process was to me. I wished I could tell them that it was *them* making it hard for me in those very moments. I wished I could ask them to just treat me as they normally would and to stop pushing drinks on me.

I didn't say any of that though; instead I pushed thought.

I had read somewhere quite extensively about how getting through a drinking event while sober, is really just a decision you have to *make*. I had gathered a lot of online advice on how to navigate the first few sober events in recovery.

One particular snippet of advice that I liked very much, was to treat the event just like an experiment. The key objectives in the experiment are to investigate, monitor, and report the findings. If you are going to try this out, I would recommend that you spend a bit of time acquiring the right mindset before the event. Make sure that you are fully on board with the idea of attending the event to simply observe and monitor *without* drinking.

The entire purpose of this method is to learn more about the effect of alcohol on the people around you and to see firsthand (sober) what it does to people physically, mentally, and emotionally. Essentially, it serves to show you what you are *not* missing. It's to prove to you that being sober puts you in a far better position in life.

I didn't give much thought to the advice when I initially read it, but while sitting 40-minutes into a drinking session as the only sober person in the room, I decided it was worth a try. I decided I would observe the evening and make mental notes of what stood out to me. I actually took a few sneaky photos and videos too, which strangely gave me something to do for the evening. No one was shoving a drink in my hand while posing for the camera or acting somewhat deluded for a video capture. I ignored the comments about my fizzy water good-naturedly and tried to get into the conversation as I usually would.

To my surprise, people only really harped on about it if it seemed to be bothering me. When I shrugged off comments and laughed along, they seemed to get bored and focus more on their own mission: drinking. I noticed that people were just talking rubbish and acting silly – that's how it appeared to me. Sitting there in that pub I realized something quite profound. I started to understand that the tipsy feeling I enjoyed so much just before I accidentally fell into full binge mode, was merely an illusion.

You are probably wondering how I came to this fantastical sounding conclusion. Well, I remember going to many pub days just like that one. When I think back on them, I fondly remember them being spans of fun. I remember them being "brilliant" and something I looked forward to, because they were so entertaining and enjoyable. I realize now that they were just average afternoons packed with average conversation, average entertainment, and the real star of show; alcohol.

It turns out that alcohol made me *think* I was having far more fun than I actually was. Have you ever taken the time to watch a drinker in action? Chances are that they are whooping with happiness and excitement at the most mundane or ordinary things. They aren't being exposed to anything that you aren't, yet they are behaving as if their experience of it is far more exciting than yours (the sober person). You might be listening to the same music or participating in the same conversation, yet they have the sense that they are having the time of their life when you are experiencing it as it is: normal. Why is that, when in reality they are having just the same experience as you, except they are wobbly on their feet and a lot louder? You are both in that moment together. They are having the exact same amount of "fun" as you are, except the alcohol gives them the impression/illusion that they are having far more fun. It's not real. It's an illusion. The realization of this really hit me.

While just watching what was going on around me, it was surprising to see just how often people repeated themselves or told the same story/joke over again. More surprising was that the group found the same jokes and stories highly entertaining and interesting each time.

It appeared as if everyone was laughing at jokes that made no sense and Kate kept chipping in on a conversation I was having with Barry, but was totally off topic. She would throw her head back and laugh, agreeing with us. It was obvious she had no real clue what we were talking about. It was quite interesting to see that a part of her brain had definitely shut off. It just was not computing the information as it should have been and in the end, her brain was playing some sort of broken telephone with her. I wondered for a bit if she would remember the conversation in the future and be somewhat confused, or if she would just completely forget it.

After a few hours – I'd say in the second hour, the slurring began. People's faces became sort of greasy/sweaty/shiny and their eyes started looking droopy. I remember snapping a few pictures of us all, for the purpose of my own investigation. These pictures were scrutinized the next day and I decided that drunk doesn't look good on *anyone*.

People's breaths were foul and the stumble-around walking was amusing to some degree, but not really attractive. One of the guys kept hiking his trousers up and trying to stuff his shirt back into them, but it wasn't working out and he looked super sloppy. People were gossiping louder than they realized and one friend, who I felt quite embarrassed for, because this is something I often used to do, was telling people things that were far too personal about herself. I knew she would regret it later.

One of the couple's, Liza and Harry, got into a heated argument, which sent Liza speeding off to the bathroom in tears. I don't think I could imagine Liza and Harry disregarding each other's feelings in this way if they were sober. I wondered how deep the hurt would go subconsciously and if it would have a future impact on their relationship. Harry of course, decided the best way to deal with it was to order the guys another round or 3 of shots. The girls ambled to the bathrooms to console Liza and there I sat, feeling quite at a loss. Don't get me wrong. I wasn't judging. Who am I to judge? I was probably the worst of this lot before my sudden desire to get sober. But I did feel very alone as the chaos unfolded around me. All I can say is; what an eye-opener!

The good news is that I got through that afternoon and evening without drinking, which was my first big sober win. My experiment's observations also bore new depth, when I heard Kev chatting to his friends about it a few days later. I couldn't help but puzzle at how much fun he *thought* he had. I was there – I know for a fact that he wasn't having quite as much fun as he seemed to be remembering. The thing is; he didn't know that because alcohol was clouding his judgement and giving him false feelings of happiness at the time.

I feel like that afternoon at the pub shone a spotlight on alcohol for me. It was like a great realization had come and now I had the knowledge I needed to take the next step. I had the strength to make better decisions for myself based on what I had learned. It was like I knew something everyone else didn't. Like I had woken up in a group of hypnotized people and was the only one awake – or the only one willing to be awake – and now I had the chance to escape.

To put the realizations about alcohol to good use in my recovery, I thought of alcohol in a different light. Have you dated someone or been friends with someone and suddenly wanted nothing to do with them? Perhaps you got to know them a bit better and they weren't quite who you thought they were. When we learn something we don't like about someone, or we find out that someone isn't honest or can't be trusted, or even if we think that they will hurt us; we walk away, don't we? We end the relationship. It's how we protect ourselves and ensure that we only get close to people who share our values. Essentially, we want to make connections with people who are good for us. Well, most of us do at least.

That's sort of what happened between me and alcohol.

It was like I was dating alcohol and had this concept in my mind that alcohol (the love of my life) was fun, exciting, and had my best interests at heart. But then one day I found out that alcohol wasn't quite the partner I thought it was. Instead, it was lying to me, cheating on me, or trying to hurt me/sabotage me. It was like one day I found out that our "relationship" was actually false. Suddenly I truly *saw* alcohol for who/what it is/was. I wasn't impressed. In fact, I felt a little disgusted. I wanted to break free from this toxic relationship. I wanted to break up with alcohol.

This realization and way of thinking really helped me in my sobriety. In fact, I believe it was one of the most valuable exercises I have ever done.

THE LIE

Something I know about alcohol is that it makes me deceitful. I wouldn't consider myself a deceitful person by nature. When I am sober, I tell the truth, even if it will get me in trouble.

I noticed that when I was binge-drinking, I would often lie. It wasn't always a big whopper, but there generally seemed to be some level of deceit from time to time. Sometimes I would talk rubbish or tell stories that weren't true. I distinctly remember my dad doing the very same thing and it seemed to make him quite popular amongst his drinking buddies. Did I pick this up from *him,* or was it alcohol that provided me with this particular talent? I believe it was alcohol, as now that I'm sober, my deceitful days seem to be behind me.

Trust me; being truthful is a much simpler and happier way to live.

Let's rewind a few years, prior to moving in with Kev and getting sober.

I feel the vibration of something buzzing next to me and for a few moments everything feels peaceful and fine. I'm vaguely aware that the world is already hard at work, as I can hear

cars and people doing buzzing about outside.
Because of the noise of the day, I begin to
surface. I let the moment settle and then
reality hits me. Crap!

My phone is vibrating and the screen says
"Kev". Shit, shit, shit. Reality is hitting me like
a ton of bricks as I squint through my semi
glued-shut eyelids. What have I done?! I
whisper this to myself in an exasperated tone.

"What. Have. I. Done?!"

I am lying on-top of the bedding in my
apartment and next to me is a man who is
definitely *not* Kevin. Given that he is away on
contract – this was before we decided to live
together - that's obvious, but this really
shouldn't be happening. I am instantly riddled
with guilt.

I know that nothing happened, but I do a full
body check anyway. I pat myself down with one
hand while I lie there. I am fully clothed
including my boots, jacket and scarf from last
night, which sends a stifled sense of relief
through my body. At least *that* isn't a problem I
have to worry about! It doesn't quell my
anxiety much though. The mere act of lying
next to this man is a betrayal of inexplicable

proportions to Kev. I know this in my heart. I personally cannot abide lies and deceit when it comes to matters of the heart. This situation would fall perfectly into that category.

I am infinitely aware of just how much I would hate it, if roles were reversed. Doing role reversal is actually a good tactic to apply when you are trying to get sober. Before you reach for that drink, tell a lie, get deceitful, or hide something; ask yourself how you would feel and react, if this very thing was being done to you by your partner, child, or loved one. It might make you rethink that action. I felt an uncomfortable clutch within the contents of my stomach.

What if Kevin spent last night out of his mind drunk, sleeping next to another woman? How would I feel if he had lied to me about his whereabouts, what time he got home, or that he had another woman at his house? Would I stick around? The answer to that is no - I would consider it a major betrayal and I certainly wouldn't be able to trust him, even if he told me that "nothing happened". You don't end up taking someone home under "nothing happened" circumstances, when blind drunk.

My mouth is so dry that my tongue scrapes the surface of my palate. The hangover has already hit me full force, but the feelings of guilt are outshining it and forcing me into action.

"Who's Kevin?" he asks.

Next to me lies Ray; my ex from several years ago. Not only does he *not* know Kevin, because we have been out of touch for many years, but he actually doesn't know *me* anymore. He is basically a stranger. I remember thinking that last night. *This isn't the Ray I remember*, but I was so drunk that it didn't niggle at me too much.

I peep at my mobile phone and notice that Kevin has phoned me 7 times. 7 missed calls that started at 8pm last night, with the last one being at 5am. It's now 8am and he is calling again. Shit! It seems like the perfect time to get all of the known profanities out there. I want to scream, punch a wall, and roll around on the floor - sheer child-like tantrum style.

I desperately want to answer Kev's messages and phone call, but I don't want to lie to him in front of a witness; particularly *this* witness. And if I am honest, what would I even say?

"You need to go now, Ray" I say as carefree-ly as I can, completely ignoring his enquiry about the "Kev" who is calling me.

He doesn't reply and seems to be set on lying there, while I start to feel increasingly uncomfortable.

"I need to get to work", I prompt him with a hint of irritation in my voice. I immediately think about work. I have a good job where I am the actual supervising manager and I haven't turned up. The irony hangs thick in the air as I realize that I clearly need a little supervision myself! I shake the thought off and try focus on what's important: getting Ray out of my apartment!

Ray jumps into action, noting the urgency in my voice. He isn't going to push it with me it seems and I am inwardly grateful for this small mercy the universe seems to have flung at me. I don't deserve it though. I deserve every inch of discomfort the situation gives me. I keep thinking this as I walk briskly towards the lounge. Here his things are strewn about and a half-finished bottle of wine sits on the table as if sneering at me.

I have a flashback to pouring more wine when I got home last night. What was I even thinking? Was I really thinking that the party must go on? Really? Argh! What on earth will I say to Kev? I start to get a bit paranoid that Kev will arrive at my door any minute. Ridiculous considering he is a 9-hour drive away, but that doesn't stop me from getting fidgety while I wait. I am hanging around the door irritably waiting for him to grab all his belongings. He seems to be taking an eternity to do trivial things, like lace up his shoes and have a sip of water. I want to scream.

"I *really* need to get going" I say again in a more pointed and semi-annoyed manner.

He jolts his head up from intense shoe-lacing and scurries around gathering the last of his things. He tries to kiss me on his way past, which I skillfully duck away from. I don't take offense that he tried this. This is entirely my fault. I realize how an ex-boyfriend, who I brought home after a night of binge-drinking, might think I was revisiting feelings for him. I shew him out the door and promise to call him later - much later and only "if there's time during work". I cannot even begin to think about how I am going to fix *this* mess. All I want is for him to be out the door, in his car, and on his way to anywhere else, but here.

As he leaves, I turn my attention to my phone. So much time has passed and I am aware that it is not going to be easy for me to get any sympathy from Kev. I can't avoid it. I close my eyes tight and allow a full-body cringe to shoot through me. I don't want to deal with this now. I want to cry and I do. With tears streaming down my face, I pensively open Kevin's messages. The last one sent at 3.45am says "Jen, you told me you went home at 7.30pm. You aren't at home and you aren't answering your phone. Donald swears he saw you out at the Excited-Gecko after midnight. I don't know what to think anymore. Who is he Jen?"

All I can think of is more curse words in my head. On repeat!

The truth is that this didn't happen because I wanted to, or had the intention to, cheat on Kev. This happened because of alcohol. Good old alcohol pretending to be my friend, but instead luring me into sticky situations that I am left to deal with alone, when the happy buzz wears off.

This happened because I share a past with Raymond and after a few glasses of wine and shots, suddenly it seemed like the most comforting and entertaining thing in the world to catch up with him. This happened because alcohol (and my need to binge on it) sometimes makes me deceitful. It makes me lie about how much I have had to drink, where I am, what time I get home, and who I'm out with. Of course, all of these lies were made a little easier by the fact that Kev is away on contract and unable to confirm anything. *Trust – not just a 5 letter word* – I think this to myself. Kev is willfully giving me trust, each and every day that he is away. And trust seems to be something that I'm willing to break, when I am paired up with alcohol for an evening. They do say ignorance is bliss don't they? Well that's how my mind thinks when I am drunk!

Last night I lied to Kevin – I think that much is obvious by now. I said I was heading home to eat and watch TV at 7.30pm, because I didn't think he would be able to handle the truth. I was drinking with my ex, who I had unexpectedly run into at the pub, while having after-work drinks with the usual bar crowd.

I had only intended on having one or two on the way home, but I should have known better.

It never really happens like that does it? One or two on the way home from work always becomes three, or four. And if you are anything like me and my dad, somewhere along the line you lose count and become someone else. I wish I could say that this was the first time I had unleashed the deceitful alcohol beast, but it wasn't.

I had stayed out far later than Kev approved of before and gotten fall down drunk. However, this was the first time that another man had ever been a proponent. This was new and had the potential to cause *real* destruction.

After I bumped into Ray, already buzzing and happy, I decided that it would be easier to *say* that I was heading home. Instead, I would just spend some time with Ray and head home in an hour or two. What harm could it cause, right? Instead of going home, I headed to a bar where people didn't really know me. This meant that Raymond and I could party the night away, without being spotted by those who might know both me and Kev. I hate the fact that I was thinking that way, but I have to be honest about it. I loathe the fact that I was *that* person.

I wanted a party and party we did. In fact, we

drank the bar (well, nearly) and then we headed on to a late night bar called Excited-Gecko, which stays open until 5am. It's not the type of place a girl in a serious relationship should find herself, especially without her other half. It's the kind of place where relationships and good intentions go to die. It's the kind of place my dad would keep a bar stool warm, while mum was home flustering over us girls, cooking dinner, and trying to make a nice home for him. It draws people in, lures them from their families and loved ones, just with the promise of a glass of *magic* liquid.

This particular pub is the type of place you never really admit to going to. During the daylight hours, no one goes there for fear of realizing the true depravity and debauchery of the joint. It's dark, it's dingy, and the scourge of humanity seems to lurk in every corner, alley, passage way, and toilet cubicle.

There's an unspoken understanding that what happens at Excited-Gecko stays at Excited-Gecko. If you see someone you know there, you might joke about it at the time, but it generally doesn't get mentioned after that. I must admit, I didn't even notice Donald there. I was, by that stage, far too drunk to be recognizing people in a smoky, dimly lit pub, which was to my detriment, obviously.

I drank, I danced, and I flirted a bit. Astoundingly, I do remember thinking at times along the lines of "should I have another drink or just call it a night" and "this is pointless". And then I took another man home. That's the real clincher, isn't it? My love of alcohol had yet again put me in a position to behave in such a way that I stood to lose everything I truly loved and valued. Don't get me wrong; I hadn't hooked up or had sex with this man, but that didn't seem to make the betrayal any less severe. I had told a handful of lies and I had withheld information. And most of these revolved around alcohol and another man.

If I was on the receiving end of this behavior or treatment, Kev and I would be over. Trust would be broken. I was nervous, but it was time to face the music.

While scrolling through Kev's messages, nervously planning my reply, a new message pops up from Raymond; "Last night was fun. We should do it again".

I groan internally and quickly type a short-hand desperate lie to Kev, to make it sound like I am too busy for insecurity.

"Power was off when I got home last night and my phone died. Definitely wasn't at Excited-Gecko. LOL. Early start today – chat later. Love you".

That lie was one of the biggest mistakes I could have made. It taught me a valuable lesson about lying. The instant gratification you get is short lived. A lie will *always* catch up with you. Kevin's reply came back quickly, like he was just waiting to send it. Serves me right I guess. It was certainly an unexpected reply and took my breath away – not in a good way. There on my screen I was staring down at a picture of me dancing far too closely and looking drunk-out-of-my-bracket, with Raymond.

"Would you like to see the video too?" he asked.

Kev had tested me and I had failed. I could have been honest and maybe the outcome would have been different, but I had chosen a different path and my fate was sealed. This wasn't just a blip in our relationship. It all but brought it to its knees.

Consequences Beat Harder Than Hangovers

Hangovers are one thing. They arrive in all their glory, they tear you apart, and they leave you bare, but then they dissipate. They are temporary. Consequences on the other hand are permanent. Consequences are quite different in that they can arrive demurely, but they cannot be budged. They don't go away the next day. In fact, they can stay with you for years, tearing you apart from within. The consequences of that night out and sleep over with Ray certainly did that.

And Then He Was Gone

And just like that, Kevin was gone. This wasn't the first lie I had told Kevin about alcohol, but I think the fact that another man was included in the lie, drove him to the precipice of our end – and then he jumped right off.

What I feared had come to fruition, finally. Kev had realized that I am not worth it and he had left me. I let this pitiful thinking consume me for quite some time. It was easier than being realistic. It was easier than admitting that Kev couldn't handle my constant drinking-related dramas and I had brought this separation on myself, not because I wasn't worth it, but because of my drinking behavior.

Kev didn't want to keep tabs on his girlfriend. He didn't want to worry all night about where she was. He didn't want his friends telling him about her betrayals. He didn't want to listen to the lies dripping from my lips like sweet, toxic nectar.

He wanted stability in his relationship. He wanted honesty. He wanted to be the only guy for me. He wanted to mean more than my regular binge nights out. He wanted me to choose us over the tears, drama, lies, or debilitating hangovers that alcohol only had to offer. I always chose alcohol even though I wanted to choose Kev. I had certainly delivered him the wrong mixed message with my behavior that night, along with all the drinking nights without him that had preceded it.

No amount of desperate messaging could get Kev to respond to me. In a way I was relieved that I didn't have to explain how that night happened in the first place. I would never have to admit that Ray had slept at my house, right next to me. It wouldn't have mattered that sex didn't happen, because who would believe that? It would be seen as yet another lie and because of that; I accepted guilt.

Kev's silence was deafening.

A week passed and I sought out bottle of wine after bottle of wine, to drown my sorrows. I lapsed into the most self-destructive binge drinking of my life. I visited every bar and pub I could, just to keep myself drunk enough not to care. Never once taking the time to realize that the very thing I was doing, was the very thing that got us into this unwanted separation in the first place. If only I had realized it. If only I could assign the blame and make a better decision for myself.

And then you will never guess who was there like a knight in shining armor to save the day; yes, it was Raymond.

RAYMOND

Let me tell you something about Raymond. Looking back, I believe he was one of the reasons why my binge drinking spiraled so out of control in the very beginning. The beginning of my spiraling started a number of years before I met Kev. This was a pivotal time in my life.

It was the year 2000-and-something and I had met the man of my dreams, or so I thought. I met him at a 'band night' at a local bar and it was his wit, sense of humor and intelligence that really snagged me. Raymond was certainly a popular guy, but not in the "jock" kind of way. Instead, people liked him because he was genuine, he was intelligent, and he was witty. He was stable, kind, caring and my family absolutely adored him – keep in mind that you never really know someone.

Our relationship moved fairly quickly. After just 8 months of seeing each other, we were living together. Within the first year and a half of our relationship, we were already engaged. It was an exciting time to say the least and I thought I had actually landed snugly into my big-yard-with-white-picket-fence-and-two-perfect-kids situation. How lucky I felt. Everything seemed to happen so easily and naturally.

We had a lovely home complete with 3 dogs, 2 cats, a big open space, and as much creativity as I wanted to bring to the home (which was a lot). We had plenty of social evenings at our house, and nights out at the pub with Ray's friends, who were great.

I actually felt complete in those days and I know this, because that's the last time I remember feeling balanced, before now. And then it all changed. We realized that I was pregnant quite soon after moving in together. We were thrilled even though we weren't married yet and our families had their judgements on that.

Our lives just seemed so perfect and a baby on the way just seemed to complete the picture. I can confirm that we were genuinely in love. We were so excited about the arrival of our little bundle of joy that we immediately began planning. We had long discussions about names, we started buying babies goodies, and we had started sorting out the spare room, which would no longer be spare.

It wasn't meant to be though as one afternoon, 5 months into my pregnancy and with absolutely no warning, I suffered a miscarriage. My world shattered around me with the shards falling into me and shredding my heart and soul into tiny little pieces. I cannot begin to express the pain that the loss unleashed on me. I couldn't tell day from night, I couldn't imagine a future, and I didn't know what to do with myself. I felt numb.

The depression and sense of loss was an experience that I can't quite equate to anything else I have ever felt. It lingered. It affected me deeply. It dug deep into the crevices of my soul in search of sensitive places to dig its claws into. One moment I was okay and the next I wasn't. For several weeks, people treated me like a delicate flower. I felt like a crushed flower. I didn't know how to help myself and everyone's awkwardness was making it worse.

Looking back, I remember that my "party-party" mood had taken a dip. My mind was consumed with grief and I wasn't fully aware of how this was affecting those around me. Grief is like a dark cloak that will engulf you. At first, it leaves a peep hole so you can see the light, but if you don't actively work to relieve the tight grip that dark cloak has on you, the peep hole can close and you feel lost inside; absorbed by the utter nothingness of the darkness around you.

Grief can take a grip on you so strong that sometimes you need a little help to break free from it. I didn't have that help and I don't think that Ray quite knew how to handle it. He was putting in extra hours at work and staying out far later than usual. I didn't blame him. In a way, I realized that miscarriages can be an emotional sense of loss for the mom and dad, and so I thought it best to give him some space.

I don't want to get too much into those days, as it's a scar I am scared to scratch open again. My soul still aches.

It took more than just a few weeks for me to break through the cloud that was hovering over me, but it slowly started to clear. I felt like I was just coming out of my haze of depression and feeling like myself again; a mere 6 months before our planned wedding date. I felt relieved and I wanted to get back to life again and the best way I knew how was to start throwing myself back into our/my normal lifestyle.

I wouldn't say that things just snapped back to normal, but some semblance of normality seemed to return to our lives, when I actively started working through my grief and dealing with the reality of what had happened. I had to go on. I couldn't stagnate. I made a choice to keep living - and I started doing that for me and for us.

I started connecting with our friends again, Ray was reporting home for dinner a little earlier, and our lives seemed to pick up where they had left off (of course with sadness in our hearts).

Just when I felt like I could breathe again, like a cruel joke, life delivered me a curve ball that I didn't know what to do with. And the messenger was my best friend Myah.

It all began with a message asking me to join her for a coffee. An innocent text message was the start to a hellish nightmare I would never wish on anyone else.

When the message arrived, it was like I had a gut feel about it. First off, I knew it was something serious, because there was no call for wine – but keep in mind that my binge drinking hadn't quite got out of control at that point. I could do coffee.

In the lead up to our coffee date I just *knew* bad news was coming. I even mentioned my bad feeling to Ray the evening before our coffee date and to this day I marvel at how detached he was from the situation. In hindsight, that should have told me everything I needed to know about him, but sometimes you are too close to the picture to actually *see* it. He said I was probably reading into things too much. I probably should have noticed how engrossed he was with text messaging that night and how on edge he seemed from the moment I mentioned my coffee date with Myah, right up until I left for the actual meet up. Why didn't I question this? Why did I let this happen right under my nose? I guess I was putting that 5 letter word into action: trust.

That afternoon, with pictures of my wedding dress and seating plans tucked under my arm, I ventured to meet Myah and face one of the most difficult moments of my life!

I remember sitting awkwardly at the table waiting for her to arrive and being acutely aware of her face pulling into a sad scowl as she walked in. As she sat down, I apologized for being so absent over the last few months and immediately launched into telling her about my new found excitement for the wedding plans. She interjected suddenly as if unable to hold it in any longer.

I suppose I don't blame her. Sometimes you just have to get the bad news out. It's like you have to expel it from you and then try to get as far away from it as possible.

"I'm pregnant", she said.

When I think about, I am transported back in time right to that moment. It's like I am reliving it every time I think about it.

I take a deep breath in. I want to be selfish and annoyed and leave, but I catch myself. Now is not the time to be selfish. Now is the time to be a friend. Now is the time to be the type of person that puts her own pain aside to celebrate the joys of someone you love. I belie my true feelings and smile warmly.

"Oh, wow!" I say. "I can see why you were afraid to tell me, but don't be My! That's great news! Who is the lucky guy?"

I didn't remember Myah being in a relationship, could this be a one night stand?

My mind runs wild and I start suggesting possible "lucky guys" and wiggle my eyebrows, trying to get her excited and into her own big moment. It doesn't seem to work and I am confused. I don't quite know what is going on, but I start to feel uncomfortable. I stop mid-sentence and look at her.

"What is going on, Myah?" I ask and she proceeds to look terrified.

I say something along the lines of "If there's no dad, that's cool. We can raise kiddo together and be like one of those weird hippy communities. They say it takes a village to raise a child!"

My joke goes unnoticed.

And then her reply was to unleash a cry. It was a strange cry. One I didn't understand at the time, but something inside me felt so sad and helpless. It was the type of cry that eases out from the center of someone's soul unchecked. It wasn't loud, it wasn't hard. It was just so sincere that I started to cry with her.

"It's Raymond's".

LIFE GOES ON; LIKE IT OR NOT

I didn't see Raymond after meeting Myah for coffee that afternoon. I knew in my heart that it was broken and couldn't be fixed. I couldn't see myself trying to make the relationship work, especially after losing my own baby. I couldn't bear to watch *their* baby grow. I couldn't forgive him.

My brain could not make sense of it and my heart was aching.

Of course I saw him physically when I got home, but I never actually spoke to him. I remember giving him the ring back and packing my things to go stay with Jo, but I don't really have much recollection of how it all played out. I know there was no begging on his part and there were no messages sent back and forth between us after I left that night. It was like the finality of the situation was severe enough for both parties to avoid all forms of negotiation.

If I think carefully about that time in my life, it almost perfectly coincides with the start of my binge-drinking career. Look, I always had a little too much alcohol before that. Alcohol was a massive part of my life, but I believe it became truly problematic at this point.

I am careful not to blame anyone or the situation for my problematic binge drinking, but it's hard to overlook that this period of my life was an undoubted trigger for the type of drinker I became. My recent miscarriage, my fiancé getting my best friend pregnant, the end of my engagement, moving out of my perfect life - I took all of these things as enough reason to start drinking a lot more and a lot harder.

After that, I remember drinking my way through various house-share scenarios, feeling sorry for myself a *lot,* and only connecting with people on a surface level for a drink – never anything more. Alcohol was my friend. Alcohol I could trust and people just weren't worth it. I didn't want to open myself up to people who could hurt me again and so I pushed everyone so far away that I lost touch with my ability to actually *make* friends eventually.

Now, several years on, I was faced with Raymond again. It all came down to a random bump-in at the pub while I was out drinking. It might not have even happened if I had not been drinking, or if Kev was in town. I wouldn't have had much interest in Ray. I would have clearly remembered the pain he caused me and moved on.

I had been best friends with alcohol ever since Ray and Myah's dirty little secret got out the bag. You would think I would steer clear of reopening that chapter in my story, but I didn't. Alcohol was making the decisions that night. If alcohol was really the best friend I thought it was, it would have walked me right out of that pub door and sent me home. Yet it didn't.

At the time, my drunk mind felt it was only natural to be interested in what happened in the story of Raymond, after I exited stage left (at rapid speed) all those years ago. That's where the drinking began that fateful night of the lie I told Kev. He had told me all about Myah being in and out of a mental health institution and about their child who had suffered because of the terrible relationship they had. I will never know what the real truth is there, as I have never spoken to Myah about. His story told a tale of them getting married and then divorced and relinquishing parental custody to his parents. Raegan, the poor child caught in the middle of this saw him every second weekend.

I might have been intrigued by Raymond that night, but I knew where my heart was. I knew I had something in Kev that I couldn't get in Ray. And then what did I do? Well, you already know; I messed up and lost Kev. Thanks alcohol. Thanks drunk decision-making.

This is just one fine example of how alcohol makes you think you are having the time of your life, while you are screwing up everything that's important to you. Alcohol will make you think that it can be a good stand in for love and solid relationships. If alcohol ever makes you believe that, know this; it's lying!

When Kev decided to freeze me out, it took weeks for me to accept it, even though I truly believe I deserved it. I sent a plethora of messages, voicemails, and online posts that undoubtedly made me look crazy.

I begged. I pleaded. I tried to explain what happened that night, which only made it worse, I'm sure. And then one day I stopped. I stopped feeling sad and started feeling indignant and mad instead.

Wine, my dear old friend, had a lot to do with that. I found I would send the most messages to Kev when I was drunk. They were mean spirited, ridiculous, and immature. I would strongly recommend against doing this – it only caused more damage.

I decided to hop off the moping train and get back out there, with my best friend, booze. And then I fell right back into the arms of Raymond. Oh dear Jen, just another *big* mistake.

The night I let Ray back into my life, I was essentially opening up a huge can of worms. And I am not talking about those cute wriggly worms that aerate your veggie garden soil and serve a purpose in your life. I am talking about flesh-eating worms that destroy everything in your life.

As it turned out, Raymond had changed over the years. He was no longer the happy-go-lucky guy he used to be and he held onto me with a vice grip that made me want to just get away.

It took about a week or two for me to notice that he was controlling, intense, and fearful. Maybe it's because his last serious relationship (Myah) was built on instability and mistrust. Maybe it's because he had gone through so much in the years we had been apart, but Ray just wasn't Ray. Dating him was a nightmare.

He questioned my every move (my wine drinking included), he checked my phone messages when I wasn't in the room, and he contacted Kevin to tell him to never speak to me again as I was his property. Unbeknown to him, Kev didn't want a shred of me anyway, but it did make Kev think there was a whole lot more to that night of the lie. I am ashamed to admit that his controlling behavior only inspired me to kick my drinking up a few notches.

They say that sometimes people are just bad for each other and I believe that now. My "take two" relationship with Raymond has taught me a lot about life. Perhaps back then I was trying to defy destiny when there was a real reason Ray and I never worked out.

At that particular stage in my life, my already-acquired binge drinking habit was strengthening, morphing, and changing me into an unstoppable monster. I wasn't fun to be out with anymore. I was definitely *not* the life and soul of the party. If I was, then the party was a sad, depressed, and angry heart and soul in deed!

I would drink to the point of crying. Yes, I was *that* person at a pub, party, or barbecue. My fears and frustrations would tumble out of me in front of people who didn't need or want to hear about them. And let's not forget that I would stumble my way through the evenings while out, tripping over my own feet and ill-fitting emotions. The stress of what was happening with Ray, and the fact that I knew I was *meant to be* with Kev, was eating me up inside. It was gnawing away at my mind, heart and soul. I felt trapped and only alcohol provided me with some reprieve. Only it wasn't reprieve. It was essentially tearing me apart, bit by bit, moment by moment, and sip by sip.

I spent most days arguing with Ray, which shouldn't come as much of a surprise. After all, we did have a cancelled wedding and a pregnant best friend in our past. The nights were spent drinking myself into a false happy oblivion. I had no idea how far I had fallen into the clutches of alcoholism, but I did know something that I desperately wanted to change. I knew I was frightfully unhappy and that I needed to get away.

This man I was with was causing me to fall apart for the *second* time in my life. Well, to be honest, not all the blame can be assigned to Ray. The unending bottles of wine and nights out wasting time, money, and myself, were also a great contributor to my distress.

I had subsequently lost my job. Luckily, or should I say thankfully, this was not due to drinking, but rather due to retrenchments at the time. As a result, I had to seek out immediate part time work until I found a better job. I started working part time at the local bar. I had rent and bills to pay after all. Or did I really just want to be in a convenient place to drink every day of my life? All I know now is that it was a really bad idea. I was literally blurring through each and every day (and night) and had become an outer shell of the person I used to be. If you had seen me, you would have been shocked. I wasn't eating right, I was drinking in excess, and my variety of "friends" was a selection of people you wouldn't want your kids to hang out with.

This went on for quite some time. I even remember that an old friend approached me once while I was at work in the bar. Her concern seemed genuine and I wish I had taken her sage advice a little more seriously. She told me I was portraying myself in a bad light by always being out, drunk and fighting with Ray. She said I was a mess and should consider getting some help. She told me Ray wasn't who he used to be and I should be careful. I didn't really know what that meant on a deeper level, although I knew that Ray had changed a *lot*. After all, that's why we were fighting so much. She told me that no man can make me complete (or a bottle of wine) and I should look after my own health more.

I think I mistook her advice a little. I should have taken hold of my life and ditched the bad job and booze addiction, but instead, I felt like I had a breath of clarity. I thought I knew what I had to do. I had to end it with Raymond. Of course, that's not what you expected. The correct thing to do would be to end my relationship with alcohol, pull myself together *and* end my relationship with Ray, but I wasn't ready yet. It was easier to blame my poor life situation on Ray – and I did.

The day I ended it with Raymond was horrendous. I was suffering the worst hangover of my life and was more miserable than usual. The same old argument had come up last night. I couldn't understand why Ray had married Myah so soon after he was meant to marry me. I wanted to know if he gave her the same ring – the one I gave back. Why this fight was still relevant, only alcohol will know. The argument was still ringing in my ears when Ray rocked up on my door step the following day.

He was chipper as he usually is the next day. It was as if the fights had never happened and his happy behavior often made me feel like I was going a little crazy. I often questioned if the toxicity of our relationship was just in my head. Or if I was the toxic one and Ray was being long-suffering. I also think he learned this habit of rocking up unannounced because he had that night of the lie to Kev in his mind. Was he trying to catch me out with another man over? I often asked myself this when he would suddenly arrive, even if I told him I was busy or unable to commit to plans.

He stood at my door with two coffees in his hands. I let him in and decided it was best get it out of the way right then and there. There I sat with yesterday's smudged make up, wild hair, deep-purple wine lips, a dry mouth and rasping voice. I wasted no time. I just said it. "It's over Ray".

Something in Ray's eyes changed. His happy look seemed to fade out, like a stifled yawn. He turned stony and cold. I suddenly saw some version of my dad staring back at me, but this time mum wasn't creating a barrier between us.

"Why?" he said – he didn't ask it. It sort of came out like a statement, which confused me. I could see something physically rising in him. His fists were clenched on his lap and his one leg seemed to be tapping, but really slowly, which was unnerving. This man in front of me was not Ray. He was someone else; perhaps just an angry version of him. I must admit that I didn't have much to draw from.

In our prior relationship, arguments were rare and there was never much need for anger and aggression. Perhaps I had just missed this particular behavior before? I didn't read too much into it, when I should have. This is probably why breakups are best done in public places; places that only offer only slight privacy.

I told him that our relationship was toxic and that we were just hurting each other. I told him I was embarrassed by our public behavior and that I also could never be a true stand-in mom figure for his child. I told him that our relationship just didn't feel right and that the amount of arguing was becoming exhausting. I told him I couldn't get over our past, and that I wasn't sure I wanted to. I didn't think we were a good fit and for whatever reasons, the years we had missed had caused a rift too big to bridge between us. Maybe I said too much. It was then time for his rebuttal.

It started with simple insults sent my way through tight lips and a clenched jaw. He said something along the lines of "This is why you haven't been able to meet my child. You're fucked up! You would be a terrible mother and that's why you lost ours!"

I was taken aback by such a harsh comment, but put it down to anger and hurt feelings. I tried to put my hand on his knee to show support and communicate that nothing said was meant to hurt. He pushed it aggressively off him and his top lip curled upwards and to the side in a sort of sneer. "I can't believe you, you bitch! You have been wasting my time!"

I tried to explain that sometimes people just aren't good for each other and I would rather he found happiness than to be with someone who isn't entirely committed to the future of the relationship. That seems to have been the news that sent him right over the edge. It was a slippery slope. Once he teetered over it, there was no coming back.

He grabbed my hair and pulled me backwards, so I fell to the ground. I was stunned into silence and when I wanted to scream, nothing came out of me. He bent down and gripped me half by the neck and half by the shoulder. He screamed right into my face, so close that I remember tasting his breath. It's strange the things that you remember from traumatic experiences, but that's something I remember clearly. You sometimes remember something else in the room that might be completely irrelevant. I remember seeing my sneakers by the door and just fixating on them.

"Is this what you want? You want an asshole! You want someone to keep you in line. You need someone to show you, don't you? I'm not worth it? Well, Jen, maybe you aren't worth the air you breathe!"

From there, it sort of phased into deep searing pain that first enveloped my face and then my stomach. The pounding came again, and again, and again. I don't even remember where I was in the room, how many times he hit me, or if I fought back.

All I remember is waking up in the local emergency room with swollen eyes, split lips and a body so pummeled I wasn't sure I could even move. How I looked on the outside was how I had been feeling on the inside for so long and the irony of that didn't escape me. As it turns out, the neighbors were astounded by the screams and scuffling noises from next door and had called emergency services.

When I opened my eyes, standing there next to the bed in the emergency room was, you guessed it, Kev.

Kev didn't come to sweep me off my feet or save me from Ray. No, not at all. He is a man of integrity and he is there for those he loves, even when they are wrong and messing up. And there he was, showing me that I *was* worth it and that Ray was wrong.

REBUILDING TRUST

In the days that followed, Kev was there for me, but didn't get too close, which was probably most wise on his part. I felt he was there, but I was aware that he wasn't particularly opening any doors for us. I have often thought back on that and wondered how he did it. If Kev had been seeing someone else and had lied to me, I am not sure that I would have been able to make myself so readily available to him. I knew that Kev was someone special and in many ways I felt that I didn't deserve him, even as a friend.

He visited me each day to "check on me" and slowly the topic of Raymond and what really happened that dreadful night of the lie was brought to light. Overcome with emotions I told him the story of mum and dad as well as the trauma of me, Myah and Ray. The silence had been broken and the truth, while not entirely believable to Kevin, was doing its work, unbeknown to us. It was starting to heal us, slowly but surely. It's hard to imagine being able to rebuild a relationship that was so damaged by alcohol, poor decisions, and poor communication, but you know what they say; love prevails.

When Kevin left after being in town for a week, I felt hollow. There was this sort of emptiness inside me. It was almost as if I had been in this tunnel and struggling to find my way out. I had been grappling around, aware that there was an escape route, but unable to find it. And then he pulled open the lid of the tunnel and I fell out, gasping for air. And then, he was gone. I felt utterly alone and I must admit that for several days I wallowed in self-pity. It wasn't that I wanted to get into a relationship with him again. It was just that I had missed having someone so genuinely care and be there for me. His time with me felt too brief. The enormity of how much I had lost through my poor decisions and alcohol consumption hung over me for a bit. Necessary I think.

One thing I remember very clearly is that I certainly wanted nothing to do with Raymond.

I wanted to be alone. I wanted to be okay. I wanted to get some semblance of a life that was *mine* and not linked to any man. I suppose the kind of thing that happened to me is a shock to the system and will give even the biggest binge drinkers food for thought. The physical recovery time I had to go through did me a world of good though. Pity it didn't last!

Being injured and looking like hell, I was unable to return to the bar for work. I am sure my mere appearance would put even the most seasoned drinkers off their grog. It was a relief being told to take time off to recover, because I was vaguely fearful of bumping into Raymond at the bar anyway.

As a result, I had to spend far less time in the pub and more time trying to think of innovative ways to make an income. The rent had to be paid, the dog had to be fed and unfortunately, bills were a real thing to be dealt with. I hadn't quite hit rock bottom with my finances, but it was close enough to put a healthy helping of fear into me.

Having studied web and graphic design when I left school, I decided to put it to good use by offering design services, which I could do from home. A higher power must have smiled on me, because thankfully it worked!

I got my first 2 clients within days of advertising online (thanks Gumtree!) and I was set up and ready to get going in no time at all. I didn't know it at the time, but this was the birth of my very own little freelance graphic design business. It was small and the income was mediocre, but it was mine and that was of paramount importance. Looking back, removing myself from the work scene and starting my own business – something to truly care about – really did wonders for me cutting back on drinking. Note, I said cutting back, not quitting.

During this brief period of unusual stability, Kev and I seemed to get back on track. My new found focus on living a wholesome life had put us on a better kilter and we resumed our long-distance relationship, somewhat carefully and with a healthy dose of hesitancy on Kev's part.

Thanks to my new work from home job I was now able to travel back and forth to spend a few weeks at a time with Kev. It seemed that life was on a good track with us. Until I got tired of traveling up and down and wanted more from us, I guess.

Even after all that had happened up until that point, I still didn't quite realize that I had a problem. I had a problem with alcohol. I wish I could revisit old me and shake me by the shoulders. I wish I could tell past me just how much more value I could have derived from life if I just stopped, then and there, but it wasn't quite meant to be – not quite yet.

I had not quite had the epiphany I needed to have to quit. I hadn't come round to the thinking that if alcohol had not been part of my life and if I didn't have a penchant for binge drinking, none of this would have happened in the first place. Instead I did what all drinkers do and I chalked it up to having a hard life. I didn't give much thought to the prospect of my life being hard because of *me* and the decisions I was making.

For about 3 months, I was motivated to turn my life into something of more value. I spent a lot more time at home focusing purely on exercise. I started doing home workouts that I found on YouTube, and my diet became more about eating whole foods instead of bags of chips and takeout. But then it seemed to fade a little, as new things do, and before I knew it, it had lost its luster. You know how life tends to tarnish your happy resolve? Well, that happened to me and suddenly I was ripe and ready to hit the pub again.

And so my binges, sans Kev, resumed.

SEEK & DESTROY NON-VALUE THINGS

Let's talk for a bit about the type of worlds we create for ourselves when we drink. As humans, we get to decide what type of bubble we want to live in, by how we react to the world and others around us.

By forming good relationships with people, earning respect, and being genuine, we can ensure that we live comfortable lives that we enjoy, with those closest to us. Some time ago, I created an uncomfortable world for myself by allowing my drinking to collide with what matters (or should matter).

For years now there has been an element of awkwardness between Kev's parents and me. His mother, who is the quiet type, was always hesitant of me because of my "creative" approach to life. She doesn't touch alcohol. It might not seem to be relevant, but I feel it should be said. Another thing I should mention is that I had no idea of this before I met her.

His stepdad is even more awkward than his mom, but is not nearly so meek. He will have the odd beer or whisky on occasion. His stepdad is not a big drinker by any stretch of the imagination. He only has one drink and never ventures into having two. How people get into this habit of "just one" is beyond me. It eludes me so much so that I have spent many hours, in fact entire afternoons, pondering it. I still don't have the answer.

When I first met Kev's parents, a balmy afternoon was in full swing and we were expecting them to arrive at any point. Knowing Kev to be the socially skilled person he is, I simply assumed that he came from similar people. Let the record reflect that he does not. Kevin and his parents could not be more different; polar opposites in fact. When they arrived, if I had been paying closer attention, I might have noticed that his entire demeanor changed. He went from the relaxed easy-going person I know him as and morphed into an awkward, uncomfortable and somewhat serious version of himself. I don't think I will ever get used to this version of him – but I accept it and have grown used to this around-the-family behavior.

The initial introductions were quite awkward to say the least. His mum didn't know whether to hug me or shake my hand and his stepdad seemed somewhat uncomfortable and semi mute.

I was both eager and nervous to meet them so my very first act was to usher them in and offer them a drink, while pouring myself a huge glass of wine. The drink was refused, but soon after Kev arranged them something anyway. I didn't pay much attention to the situation, other than to hear that drinks were being poured.

I was clutching my wine, which served as my security blanket; my safety net. I was fully prepared to use this glass of wine to get me in the "zone" and see me through this event. My nerves and anxiety were through the roof. At first, I wasn't aware that everyone else was drinking mere apple juice in their wine glasses. If I had known, I know for a fact that I would have thought "what a waste of a wine glass", but I also would have slowed down a little! Only after the first hour had passed, when I had relaxed to the point of laughing too loudly, oversharing information, and looking a bit lazy-eyed, it finally struck me. Everyone else was sober and I most certainly was not!

While that information should have stopped me in its tracks, I am sad to say that it didn't. The obvious solution seemed to drink more and I did. I felt embarrassed, but just couldn't stop myself. My brain said "binge" and my body listened. It wasn't all that bad. I mean I didn't dance on the table or swear at his stepdad, but my drunkenness was unmistakable and the parents left a bit earlier than I expected. I am not sure if it was my behavior that sent them packing so quickly, but I can only assume and I am fairly certain my assumptions were correct.

Unfortunately, since that first meeting, our relationship hasn't been close. I can't help but feel that if I had shown more interest in getting to know them than getting to the bottom of my wine glass, things would be a whole lot different today.

Once they had left and I resembled a sober version of myself, Kev decided to approach the subject with me. He said he never expected me to drink around his parents and so never thought to forewarn me that they did not imbibe. He said that perhaps next time, I could hold back on the drinking around the family. And so after that day, we *never* drank around the parents. In fact, we never drank at family gatherings at all after that. That didn't suit me at the time and I remember complaining on many occasions about it, but nowadays I am thankful for it.

I still feel like I have lost out on something in those relationships though – only time will tell. Perhaps as the years pass, the chance to make something of it will come up.

ALCOHOL SEEKS & DESTROYS THAT WHICH HAS MEANING

I first made the connection that alcohol was a thief of things meaningful to me, right before I decided to quit drinking. It was when Kevin came to visit me on one of his work breaks. He planned to do the trip by car, which meant that he was faced with a grueling 9-hour drive. The occasion was his birthday, which was coming up the next day.

I was absolutely elated that he had chosen to come back home for his birthday – and spend it with me. I felt special.

To prepare for the occasion, I had reached out to a drinking buddy from the pub. I asked her to join me on a mission to shop for a birthday cake, snacks, drinks, groceries, and a present. I wanted to absolutely shower him with spoils the moment he arrived at my place.

The friend, who we shall call Tamzin, agreed to join me on this mission. I remember feeling quite excited about the occasion and the fact that a drinking buddy was potentially turning into a *real friend*. This was something I really wanted in my life. She seemed just as excited at the prospect of Kev visiting as I was, which really made me happy. I was in my element!

When Tamzin arrived at my apartment, she bustled in excitedly with an already opened bottle of champagne. The pink bubbliness was enticing. "Woohoo!" she screamed as she raced up the garden path and in through my front door. "He's coming today! Time to P-A-R-T-Y!"

Her excitement engulfed me. She had a way of making things feel extra fun and that's probably why I thought we could be friends. She passed the bottle of bubbly to me and I took a sip, reveling in the fizziness as it slid down my throat and started doing its work.

Just a few more swigs later, the bottle was finished. We trashed it and headed out on our way, with the shopping list in hand. I don't know how I was so blind at the time. Maybe it's because I was on the same self-destructive path as Tamzin was, but we were and never will be good for each other. Tamzin wasn't there to be my friend. She was there to have a drinking buddy, but I only realized this too late, when far too much damage had already been done.

While already shiny-eyed tipsy, I got behind the wheel of my car and headed into the city. We had a list of items to get and I didn't have too much time as Kev was already well on his way. Our first stop was the stationery shop, to get a birthday card for him. Down the road from the stationery shop there was a cake shop, where I hoped to find a themed cake or cupcakes that would be perfect.

After taking some time selecting the birthday card, I couldn't help but notice that Tamzin was looking a little bored. I think the reality that this was an actual shopping mission was hitting her. I think she would have preferred to pop the cork on that second bottle of bubbly I saw in her handbag. My own mouth salivated at the thought and I started to feel bad for making her do this with me.

As we trundled back towards the car with a suitably hilarious birthday card stuffed into my handbag, she gave me a naughty look and suggested we "make things a bit more fun" by bar hopping along the way. My inner drunk made that decision for me in an instant. Instead of heading for the cake shop, we headed in the direction of an upmarket bar, just around the corner.

As we stepped into the entrance of the bar, that familiar comforting stale beer stench, that any barfly will recognize, hit me in the face. The dim lighting (deterring you from realizing there is a bright and beautiful world outside) lured me in. There's no denying it; I have always felt most at home on a bar stool in a dark and dingy bar. My dad had often taken me to bars and pubs with him as a child, where I sat around waiting for him to be "done" for hours on end. As a result, the easiest conversations I have ever had are with drunken people in bars.

I could feel an instant mood boost find its way into both of us as we ordered tequila shots and a glass of white wine each. I chugged the drinks back with the realization in my mind that I was running out of time. I still had time for a drink though. In fact, I was happy to *make* time.

Tamzin kept telling me that the trip to pick up the cake should be delayed, because it would melt in the car. At first I was wary, worried that we would miss closing time, but finally I agreed she was right. Instead of seeking out a cake, we headed off to go find a present first and foremost. We parked the car close to the mall and as we strolled up towards it, we passed another small bar. By this time, the alcohol was coursing through our veins and empty stomachs. Logic and clear thinking was replaced with "ooh this looks like fun" thought processes and soon prior plans were out the window.

Neither of us had ever been to this bar before, so it seemed like a good idea to go inside and check it out. I distinctly remember saying that I hope the bar would have a "good vibe". It's funny how that becomes of paramount importance when drinking. At this point, Tamzin was most animated and her stories were producing the type of belly-ache laughing I have only read about in books and seen on TV. I absolutely adored this new friend. She was great. Or was that just the alcohol doing the thinking for me? I believe now that it was. Since I quit drinking, Tamzin's contact with me has been non-existent and my messages have been ignored.

We settled onto our bar stools and started on our next round of drinks. Some friendly people from further down the bar struck up a conversation with us and from there things get a little hazy. I don't quite know what happened next. Suddenly hours had passed, it was dark outside and my list was burning a hole in my pocket. I suddenly realized that all the stores were closed and Kev's present, cake, snacks, drinks, and groceries had not been retrieved. All I had got was drunk.

I looked at everyone's faces around me and started to feel overwhelmed. I grappled around in my handbag for my mobile phone. You know that drunken rifling through a bag? That was me. Where was it?! I didn't even know what the time was.

I was acutely aware of the way my steps seemed a little stumbly. I started desperately scratching around in my handbag and patting my pockets for my mobile phone, which was only drawing more attention to me. One of the girls in the group cracked a completely unrelated joke, which sent me into an emotional state. I burst into tears thinking that she was talking about me when she wasn't. I half-realized that I had lost track of time and would appear as a completely uncaring person to Kev, which only worsened my overwhelmed emotional state. After everything I had already put him through in the past months with Ray; I was starting to panic that this may be the beginning of the end!

It was past the point of no return. It was like I was trapped in a bubble. I couldn't be drunk right now and needed to be sober, but there was nothing I could do but be drunk. I was trapped being drunk and to make things worse, I wasn't making sense.

Tamzin seemed to be laughing uncontrollably at my distress. The more I told her that we had messed up, the more she insisted that it was nothing to worry about and that I should have another drink. I flapped the list at her with only one check on it next to the "birthday card" entry. "We hash done nothingggggg" I slurred, which only sent her into another fit of hilarious laughter.

Just then, a familiar face walked into the bar and approached us. It was Kev's old work friend, David. "Are you okay love?" he asked, obviously concerned about my state. I wasn't okay. Tears were streaming down my face, I couldn't find my car keys, and the more I tried to explain why I was so upset, the more upset and illogical I become.

I think he kind of understood that I was upset about letting Kev down and he lead me away to sit with him and his girlfriend, who were having what appeared to be a calm and quiet dinner. I saw him whip out his phone and in my drunken illogical mind; I assumed he was phoning Kev who would hopefully come to meet us. The tears still streamed and I kept on sniffling in an unladylike fashion, while slumped in the chair next to them, still sipping on a beer mind you.

After what seemed like hours I finally asked him when Kev would be arriving. He looked confused and replied "Kev? I didn't know he was coming!"

All I can say is O.M.G! That sent me into a fit of distress. My crying was uncontrollable, but it seemed like the best thing to do at the time. If I was sober, I would have been mortified at the scene I was making. My shirt was untucked, my hair was a mess, and my makeup was smudged to the extent that I don't think anyone would have recognized me. I was the girl that cries in a bar. I was the girl that just couldn't handle her drink.

I bolted from the table, desperate to salvage the mess I had made of "mission spoil Kev". I found my mobile phone and keys in my handbag where they had been all along (my brain just wasn't recognizing them it seems). I stumbled outside, jammed the car keys into the lock and opened the car. I got inside and grabbed my phone out of my bag. 4 missed calls from Kev. The time was precisely

11.50pm! Kevin had been in town exactly 4-and-a-half hours and had no idea where I was. I turned the ignition on and headed in the direction of home. I know… I *know*. Driving under the influence is absolutely unacceptable and I am ashamed that it's something I did that night, but I did and I have to be accountable for it.

The messages Kev had sent me that evening, when he arrived to an empty apartment and no explanation, were first loving and then desperate. And when I arrived to find him sitting locked outside on my front doorstep, I couldn't help but feel like a complete and utter failure. I cried. I cried so hard that it felt like something inside me was trying to get out. I had let alcohol steal the entire day and it was now officially Kevin's birthday and all I had to spoil him with was me…a drunk, smelly, crying mess that had totally neglected him all night. In that moment I knew that I hated alcohol. I knew that it was a problem, but I wasn't sure if there was something I was willing to do about it.

I held up the list with one check next "birthday card" and he read it looking somewhat bewildered. He took my keys, opened the apartment door, took me inside, and made me some tea. I fell asleep on the couch before I drank it, but it was waiting next to me the next morning – a cold reminder of just how much I had messed up.

I will never forget the feeling I had after that particular mess up. I will also never forget how gracefully Kev accepted that he was not spoiled, even remotely, on his birthday. Of course, yours truly was nursing a colossal hangover that day.

When I look back on this I cannot believe how selfish alcohol made me. It made me think about me and me alone. I wanted to have a good time. I wanted to have a drink. I wanted to feel good. I wanted these selfish things so much that I would let people down and hurt them. In the end, I would feel sorry for myself. It's a very unproductive cycle, to say the least. I am so glad that my path of sobriety has changed *me* for the better. It has made me more aware of other people and how my actions play a role in their life experience. I have become far less selfish and that's a version of me that I can actually live with. I don't think that this version of me would be possible if I was still drinking.

Every year I remember how this particular birthday went for Kev. Although too little too late, I try to put a bit of extra effort into his birthdays nowadays, to make up for the past. I didn't deserve the patience and kindness he had given me on that night or on the other nights that followed.

This particular story brings me to the sensitive topic of creating distance between yourself and those who are bad for your new way of life. I know that this happened during the prime of my drinking days and not after I had made the choice to quit, but the sentiment is the same. Had I not teamed up with Tamzin on that day, chances are that I would have got a lot more done.

Yes, maybe I would have drunk alcohol that day, but I *might* have prioritized and saved my drinking for Kev's arrival. I can't blame Tamzin. I certainly can't blame her when I am the one with an alcohol addiction and only I can change that. If I hadn't been addicted to alcohol, I would never have let so many hours slip me by, just for a few drinks and meaningless banter with strangers.

But here's the thing. When you choose to get sober, there will be people who either support your efforts or work against them. I am not suggesting that we should cut out everyone from our lives, just because they drink. But if you have that one friend that can only socialize with you at a bar while throwing back countless drinks and shots, you are going to have to put that friendship on the backburner for a bit.

If you have specific people in your life that mock you or try push drinks on you even if you have explained you aren't drinking right now, you are going to have to avoid them. Try talking to them first. Tell them that you may have to avoid them if they keep pushing drinks on you, and then make the conscious decision to do just that if they don't respect your decision.

Right now you need to ensure that the relationships you develop are those that add real value to your life. If you join an online sobriety group, you might find that there are several people in your area that would love to make a new sober friend. Sober friends are hard to find, so when you do find them, hang onto them. With this new friend or group of friends, you can go shopping, go for lunch, go on hikes, picnic in the park, go to the movies and do other sober activities. You can do all of this without the fear of drinks being incorporated.

You never know, you might just make new friendships that add real value to your life!

DREAMS OF NO ESCAPE

When I mentally made the decision to quit
drinking, it became an all-consuming focus for
me. Getting sober isn't something that you can
do part-time. It becomes something you
actively put effort into every single day of your
life. I knew it would be hard and I think the
dread I held onto actually made it far harder
than it would have been. The decision weighed
on my mind heavily. I won't lie, there was an
internal conflict in my mind like never before. I
thought about my decision consistently. I
found myself unable to escape it. I was always
bargaining with myself in my mind and I think
that's because the word "forever" scared the
crap out of me. Would I really never have
another glass of wine again? How can that be!

I don't know if you have ever got so caught up
in your head before that you simply cannot do
anything. You don't know where to start with
the things you need to do and you get flustered.
That was me for a while. I felt as if my life was a
blur and all I could do was try to breathe
through my anxiety. The anxiety was high. It
was rife. It was making matters worse. In fact,
drinking was something I often did to
temporarily fend off anxiety!

What made it all the more terrifying was that I found everything about my alcoholism so deeply personal. It was so personal and intimate to me, that deciding to quit seemed like a personal injury to my very being. My problematic drinking had become a part of me. It was how I survived. It had been there for me for so many years and what's more is that it was what I turned to in happy times, sad times, and even stressful times. I knew it was destroying me, but I loved it so much that I just wanted more and more. It's like loving someone that's bad for you even though everyone in your life is warning you against him/her. For some reason, you are willing to overlook the bad and keep going. It's like staying in a relationship with someone for longer than you should, because you just can't bring yourself to break it off. I was just extending my agony by holding back and delaying my sobriety. I was putting it off time and again and I kept telling myself that "no man, you aren't *so* bad". I knew I was though. Deep down, I knew.

It was excruciating to both realize and accept that the very thing I wanted the most, was the very thing ripping my life apart. It wasn't just trying to destroy me; it was actually succeeding. Addiction is sneaky like that. You think your substance of choice is making your life better and helping you cope, when in reality, behind your back it is plotting your demise. It is slowly wrapping its roots and almost-invisible vines around your hands and feet, securing you to one spot; it's causing you to stagnate in life, and keeping you from everything you *could* be. It's pulling you down and holding you back.

You think you are in control, but the truth is that you are not. If you were in control, saying no wouldn't be so hard. Somewhere along the line, we signed a seemingly unbreakable contract with alcohol and now, it's in control. It tells us who we will spend time with, what events we go to, how we look, how much time we spend on things we really love, and what disease or mental health disorder we will get next. Alcohol decides, because we signed our power over to it. We only prove this every time we plan our weekends around drinking events, every time we are too hungover to spend quality time with our kids or partners, every time we look in the mirror and aren't happy with our belly bulge or wrinkled skin, every time we say we don't have time to exercise or participate in a hobby, and every time we fear heart disease, diabetes, and liver cancer. For me, it was time to take control of my life back, but alcohol wasn't going to just let me do that. My addiction was going to put up a fight – and it did. Alcoholism is a worthy opponent, but it's undefeatable. I learned that by finally taking the plunge and choosing to escape, rather than stay stagnant.

My obsession about my decision started filtering into every crevice of my life. Even my dreams reflected my desperation and urgency mingled with despair, panic, and excitement. I remember one particular recurring dream I had that quite unnerved me. I didn't know what it meant back then, but I do now.

In the dream I am walking barefoot through a forest and marveling at the beauty around me. I can feel the coolness of the ground beneath my feet and there's a gentle breeze blowing through my hair, which is hanging down my back and all around me. In my dream, I am the most beautiful I have ever been. I feel immensely happy. It feels as if I am on top of the world. I am picking flowers, eating berries, and being care-free.

Suddenly something underfoot stops me. It hurts and I bend down to see what it is. I am only distracted for a few minutes trying to see what has hurt me, but I can't quite figure it out.

As soon as I lift my head, it's suddenly dark around me. I can just sort of see around me, but it's not clear.

I start to feel incredibly insecure and my anxiety is rising. I feel so anxious that I want to scream but I can't, because I am in this *happy place*. Screaming doesn't seem appropriate or even possible, but the frustration is welling up inside me. There's absolutely no release and I am panicking. I stumble forward gasping for air and all the while the soft cool ground beneath my feet from before, now feels like gnarled tree roots that are writhing and squirming on the ground. With every movement it feels like ropes of sandpaper against the soft skin of my feet. Every time I take a step, tree roots curl around my ankles and legs and pull me downwards and backwards, like an anchor. It's like I am in a pit of sinking sand, except with tree roots instead of sand. The more I struggle, the stronger they pull me down and the tighter they wrap around my legs. There's an inexplicable level of desperation taking over me.

I keep pressing forward, just trying to find somewhere to stand where there are no roots. There's a stench in the air that makes me feel sick and my skin is rasping against foliage.

There are feathers of dead birds everywhere, but I don't actually see any dead birds. It's like I just *know* they are dead. It is like I am stuck in a thicket, but the tree leaves and branches aren't actually anywhere near me. I try to call out, but nothing is coming out of my mouth. I lean down and pull at the tightening roots on my legs, but this just makes thorns appear on them, which tear into my skin. I want to give up, but I also don't know if I should. Blood is trickling down my legs and I start to feel really weak and tired. I can't figure out why all of this is happening. I keep trying to figure out where I am.

I look directly ahead of me and I see a shining light at the end of the forest tunnel. I can see green grass, blue sky, and a normal world out there, but I just can't get there. I can't call for someone to help me, because my voice won't work and I can't physically reach the exit, because I am dragged down by creeping vines and tree roots. I stretch out my hands and as I do so, the air starts to get thick. I can't breathe so well. I can feel a bit of a cool breeze floating in and instinctively know that it's coming from the light at the end of the forest tunnel.

I am gasping for air in such a way that every inch of my body is heaving and every time I catch a bit of the air streaming in from the light side, I am instantly relieved, but then the suffocating begins seconds later again. I know where I need to be, but there's no escape route. I want to get there *so* badly, but all my struggling against the roots has made me get stuck. Suddenly I see a dimly lit path, my obvious escape route, unfurling ahead of me. I am excited but suddenly struck with dread because it is an extremely steep climb – it looks all uphill and I am not sure if I have the energy to make it. Before I can venture towards it though, I wake up sweating and feel outrageously anxious. It was almost as if my dreams wouldn't even let me *decide* whether or not to take that escape route.

I had this dream many times and wondered what it could mean. I even considered finding an online dream interpreter to help me figure it out, but in the end, I think the answer and understanding truly lay within me. It was only after I truly decided to commit to my sobriety body, mind, and soul that suddenly the dream started to make a little more sense to me. Now that I have a bit more understanding of how I was feeling back then, I think the dream was all about my addiction to alcohol. I think it was highlighting the fact that I allowed it to hold me back for so long. I let it keep me anchored until I eventually felt like I didn't have a choice anymore. Alcohol was doing all of the decision-making and I was just following orders. My mind was obviously telling me that there *was* an escape route for me, but it was going to be hard work. Freedom and fresh air could be mine if I was willing to put the work in and be intentional and about my transformation. I haven't had this dream in a really long time, but I don't think I will ever forget it. In fact, it inspired the very cover and title of this book.

Intentional Transformation

You might be wondering how I went from the girl that simply couldn't say no to a drink, to the person I am today. What I can tell you is that my transformation came from intent. I intentionally created a life that is better without booze and I am very keen to share *how* with you.

In the pages to follow you will find several sections dedicated to advice, guidance and stories, based on my own experience. You might find some of the sections uninteresting, boring, *or* extremely relevant to your life – whatever, the case may be; it is *your* journey and I want you to take from this book *anything* that may help you and leave behind anything that doesn't.

I wanted to keep this part vaguely separate from my story, so that while going through them, you have *my* story to reference. Knowing where I come from makes it easier to understand why I have done things the way I have.

In the final chapters you will find a section called #The Sober Project which I very strongly recommend you pay attention to, even if you skip through any of the other sections. In that section is what I believe is the secret to my sobriety. The #Sober Project is what I have

using as my secret Escape Route from booze –
and it is *really* working for me.

QUITTING FOR *ME*

It took many years of being completely and utterly oblivious to my alcohol abuse, before I noticed that there might be a problem at play. And this is the very reason why I firmly believe that the decision to quit must come from within, for *you*.

I have seen countless people in relationships trying to force their other half to see the signs, to quit the bottle, and to live a better life. I have seen these attempts fail. The problem with this is that you cannot make someone see a problem that they don't believe is there. You cannot force someone to stop drinking. They have to find a reason to quit. Someone cannot quit for *you*. Someone has to quit for themselves.

Many years of drunken oblivion passed me by during my drinking days. I often look back and wonder how much more I would have achieved in life if I was a drinker that's more like Kev, or if I just simply never drank at all. Kev might have been an enabler, but he certainly didn't deserve what I dished up to him. I am a horrible drunk and there's just no point trying to make sense of it. Brain chemistry is a tricky thing to understand, before you even start to water it down with alcohol. It's a whole lot more tricky to understand when you are tinkering with the chemicals in your head, with the chemicals in a bottle.

I know the drinking wasn't all bad when it came to me and Kev. There have been times where we have both enjoyed a great night out. We have gone home, held each other tight and slept till morning without a shred of malic between us. But there have been far more times when I have spat hatred and abuse at him. There are far more times where we have got into a row, or slept in separate beds just because alcohol had taken us to a point where we were no longer our true selves. Alcohol was always fun, to a point. Who can really say for sure how the evening is going to end when there's alcohol involved?

There's something that you need to know about alcohol and I have alluded to this earlier on in this book. Alcohol is that one bad friend that always seems to lure your into some sort of trouble. Sure, this friend is fun and exciting. For the most part it seems like harmless fun, doesn't it? But how often does that harmless fun turn into saying something you wouldn't normally say? How often do you end up getting louder and cruder as the hours drag on? How often does the fun turn into upset, hurt feelings, or an argument with a friend or a loved one? How often does that excitement lead to crying, falling over, or vomiting? How often does that fun turn into next-day illness, puffy eyes, red/grey skin, sore teeth, and a queasy stomach?

What type of "friend" gives you cancer and heart disease? Imagine you knew that hanging out with one of your friends would give you liver disease or cancer? Would you do it? Would you consistently spend time with this dangerous friend?

How about if you knew that your friend was going to embarrass you or hurt you on a night out? What if you knew that your friend was going to make you cry? What if you knew that your friend wanted to break you and your partner up? How much time would you really want to spend with this friend? The reality is that you wouldn't. You wouldn't want this type of friend in your life, would you?

If you had a human friend in your life that brought about these downfalls and discomforts consistently, would you keep them around? Would you keep giving them a call to come over just 2 days after your last unpleasant episode with them, just to repeat the process all over again? Probably not, right? So, why do we do it with alcohol? Why do we let liquid in a bottle lure us into trouble and treat us with such disrespect and disregard time and again, and never do anything about it? This thought clattered around my mind on a regular basis, especially in the days just before deciding to quit.

Food for thought, to say the least.

Houseplant Theory

Let's talk about house plants for a bit. I find
having house plants very soothing. I have
learned a lot about sobriety from the plants
that I have dotted around my home.

The sooner you learn to treat yourself like a
houseplant, the better. I contemplated this
quite a lot when I first went alcohol-free.
Someone passed the comment of "treat
yourself like a houseplant" to me as a joke one
day, but it really resonated with me. It seemed
so relevant to my recovery.

When I first quit drinking, I started thinking
about what I could do to make myself feel
better. It's hard to accept that we must now
face life without a mind-and-mood altering
chemical, shaving the edges off of life's hard or
complicated moments. I found myself Googling
a lot of things. I wanted to know what to do to
feel better and how to socialize without alcohol.
I wondered if I should pop pills, eat differently,
join a club – I am sure you know how it goes. I
often found myself looking for that magic
answer; you know, that magical natural
substance you can take *instead* of alcohol that

will provide all of the benefits and none of the bad stuff? Yup, I searched for it and I must tell you that it is a complete waste of time. That magical alternative to alcohol doesn't exist. The only true and reliable alternative is sobriety.

The reality is that everyone's recovery is different. You might need to go to a rehab facility whereas I didn't. You might need some medication to help you with the detoxing process, whereas I was able to get through without it. I can't tell you what you might need medically, but what I can tell you, is that I learned that we *all* stand to gain by treating ourselves like a houseplant.

You might be wondering what this means. Well, it basically means that you need a few physical basics to ensure that you get through this particularly crappy time. You need a few basics to make you thrive.

The start is the hardest and if you don't strategize for success, you are going to find yourself slipping backwards and with nothing to grip onto. If you have a strategy, you have *that* to grip onto.

It's hard to explain, but when I started strategizing for sober success, things started to fall into place. I had something to fall back on when things got a bit rocky or shaky.

It's kind of like training, when you start a new job. There's a "system" to learn and you undoubtedly get training for it (like reading this book for example), but then something happens that gets you flustered and suddenly you don't know what to do. You need to get your brain thinking about that training you had, but you can't without a strategy. Perhaps your strategy is to take a few deep breaths and then refer to a list of key points you have written on a post-it note and stuck to your computer, for example. That's strategizing for success in that particular scenario.

The first step in strategizing for my own success was to get myself physically healthy. When things got rocky, I wanted to have my new and healthy lifestyle to fall back on. I wanted to be able to compare how good I felt healthy to how bad I felt slipping up or hungover. I wanted my body to heal and feel energized. I wanted my body to *want* the new health I was able to give it. And that's where the houseplant theory came into action for me.

Think about it... what does a houseplant need to survive and thrive?

Keeping a house plant happy isn't rocket science. It's not an overly complicated process. First, it needs space; then it needs water, good nutrition, and a decent amount of sunshine each day. Provide all of these things and you will have a healthy and happy houseplant on your hands.

Give *yourself* these very things and you too will thrive physically. You will activate a healthier side of life within you and healing will begin.

Space

First things first; you need some space to just "be" in.

Healthy space is a good idea. A pot plant won't thrive if it's in an old pot that's too small for its root system or jammed into a pot with other plants fighting for the same resources. Much the same, if the space is unhealthy (say, by being too dark or too damp or without drainage holes), it's not going to thrive. In fact, it might die. Where you are right now in your life is something that needs close scrutiny. Your personal space is basically your pot, so try looking into ways of making your home environment healthy for your sobriety. Don't put yourself in unhealthy environments where people won't understand your new journey or don't support it. Temporarily remove yourself from any environment that may negatively impact on your sobriety. I am not suggesting you run away from your partner or family!

For me, it was all about "out with the old and in with the new". I tossed out all of the Jen-friendly alcohols. I mean, I couldn't get rid of Kevin's alcohol, but I was never one to drink beer anyway. All the wine, whiskey and tequila found its way into the bin and I replaced them with bottles of sparkling water, tonic water, alcohol-free beer and alcohol-free wine. There's even a range of alcohol-free whisky and brandy online (called Arkay) that I found, not that those were ever my drink of choice. But it's nice to know that they do exist.

I also stocked up on a few treats that were semi-healthy, so that I didn't end up giving in to the sugar and carb cravings that always seem to make an appearance when trying to quit *anything* in my life. I do snack still, but my current favorite snacks are peanut butter smeared on apple slices (why people aren't addicted to *this,* I don't know), sesame seed bars, popcorn (I bought an air popper to reduce oil), dried fruit pieces, and different flavored teas.

Making a home a healthy space is about more than what you will eat and drink. It's also about how you will make yourself comfortable during the toughest days. You know those days when you just think that it's *"just one drink"*? Well, those are the times when you need the type of space that offers you a few alternatives to this behavior. I went all out and I understand this isn't for everyone.

I invested in a few bottles of bubble bath and scented candles, because my go-to on a night when Kev has friends over for drinks, or if I am having a hard day, is to read quit lit in a bubble bath. I can quite literally spend hours doing this.

I created a long list of series on Netflix to watch instantly without having to spend hours searching for something – we all know how frustrating that can be.

I ordered a container gardening kit online, so I had something to do on warm days.

And I bought myself a yoga mat, ball, jump rope, and hula hoop so that I could start getting myself into exercise. I downloaded a list of work out videos that I could do – easy and simple for home use. I still do all of this.

Nutrition

Another thing that a houseplant needs is good nutrition. I don't recommend trying to change everything about your life when you quit drinking, so tread carefully here. If you go on a strict diet *and* get sober at the same time, it may feel like too much. No scrap that! It *will* be too much.

I personally made a few tweaks to my diet that helped me a lot. I didn't change all my meals, but I did change my breakfast. I made sure that every day started with a healthy, balanced breakfast. Muesli and plant milk, avocado on toast, fresh fruit, and cooked oats – you get the point.

Just add something healthy to your diet and that's a good step towards positive change. You can make more adjustments as you go, but don't try and be a keto champion on day 1. Take it slow and steady.

I also put myself on a vitamin B complex (great for energy by the way) and a good multivitamin. That's all – nothing more and nothing less – that's what worked for me.

Water

Another really important thing that a houseplant needs is plenty of water.

When I quit drinking, I had to get serious with myself about hydration. I wasn't very kind to my body when I was drinking. During my binge-drinking days, water was the furthest thing from my mind and the yellowish tinge to my eyes after a weekend of drinking was very telling. Nowadays, I have a new found love for water. If you can drink 4 to 6 glasses of water over the space of the day, you are doing great. They do say that 8 glasses is ideal, but I personally struggled with that.

I got myself a 1.5 liter bottle, filled it with water, and sipped consistently from it – and refilled it as I went. I still do this because I have developed a habit for sipping on water constantly throughout the day. My liver is happy and my skin has transformed to something I don't quite recognize: youthful amazing skin, even at my age! Who knew!

You might not feel like drinking water – I know I didn't – but the truth is that your body needs to hydrate in order to heal. Drinking fruit juice or sodas might be tempting, but the extra sugar might make you pick up weight, and who needs that at a time like this?

I was binge drinking at the very least 3 times a week and drinking moderately 4 times a week. It's safe to say that my liver has been overworked in its time.

Water is quite miraculous in recovery as it helps the body release toxins via the digestive system and urinary system as well as through respiration and sweating. When you are in withdrawal from alcohol, the body cycles out a lot of vital fluids while recovering and healing. Keep topping yourself up and try to keep thinking of yourself as a thirsty, growing houseplant.

Sunshine

Lastly, and most importantly, a houseplant needs plenty of sunshine in order to thrive. A houseplant will use the sunshine it gets to carry out the process of photosynthesis, which helps it grow, heal, and thrive. Humans also need sunshine.

Getting into the sun for at least 10 to 15 minutes per day can boost your vitamin D levels. Most people don't give vitamin D much thought, but it's essential for healthy teeth, bones and muscles. It's about more than that too. In fact; vitamin D can reduce the risk and effects of depression. Think of it as a dose of happiness. Right now you need that, so try to get a few rays of sunshine every single day.

I suffer from depression on and off and where I live there isn't always an abundance of sunshine, so I have always taken vitamin D supplements and made a point of getting into the sunshine whenever the opportunity presents itself.

When I started exercising, I was lucky because it was summer. I put my yoga mat on the lawn in the sun and got my Vitamin D fix that way for at least 20 minutes a day.

You can get creative about getting your vitamin D. You can pop some pills or you can spend time outside. Sit in the sun for your morning breakfast or a cup of tea. Take a stroll in the sunshine during your lunch break. Plan a picnic in the sun for the weekend. There are plenty of creative ways to get a good dose of Vitamin D. How would you like to get yours?

SOBER SOCIALS

Socializing sober seems to be a sensitive topic for a lot of people. Being the only sober person in a room can be frustrating, annoying, and boring. It also comes with a lot of responsibility.

How do you plan to handle sober socializing? Do you have a strategy? I didn't really have a strategy to begin with. I basically just bumbled my way through these occasions, which is what made them difficult. What I can tell you is that sober socializing is something of a fine art. It requires a strategy.

I know that there are hundreds of sober people out there that believe it is best not to hang out with people who drink, but for me, that didn't quite fit. I didn't want to break ties with good people because they weren't on the same path as me. I didn't feel that I was in a position to judge or exclude anyone. I had the thought in my mind that I would hate for someone to exclude me, just because I had a past with alcohol. Since moving in with Kev, he had introduced me to a lot of people who cared for me and provided valuable friendship. I had no intention of cutting them out because I was an alcoholic and they liked to drink.

I have already mentioned how I handled my first sober social at the pub with a group of friends, but that wasn't the only sober social I attended. I must admit that some have been harder to handle than others. On some occasions, it is harder resist temptation than others.

We have already discussed the idea that alcohol only provides the illusion of fun. I know, you might think "so what, it's still fun". Well it's not really. Imagine if I told you that I was going to give you a pill that made you *think* that your partner loved you, but they didn't really love you at all. Would you want to take that pill? I want you to think long and hard about that, because that's what alcohol does. It makes you *think* that you are having fun, but you aren't really.

There's another theory I have already mentioned to you, that I want you to think about right now too. Imagine you had a friend that always makes you feel bad. This friend doesn't care about your feelings and makes you become someone else when you are around her/him. You start out having fun when you spend time with this friend, but the evening always takes a dramatic or horrible turn. The next day you always feel really bad and have serious remorse for inviting her/him in the first place.

How often would you invite this friend to your social gatherings? Would you really want to invite this person to your home barbecues or to share time spent with your nearest and dearest? The reality is that you probably wouldn't want that friend around, because you know better and you want better for yourself. The reality is that alcohol is *that* friend.

This concept can be tricky to wrap your head around, because we aren't taught to think in such parallels. That doesn't mean we shouldn't. We have spent our entire lives being shown, told, and taught – by our parents, peers, and the powerful advertising spend of the alcohol industry – that alcohol is great for us. I watched alcohol destroy my parent's marriage and lives and yet somehow the only message that was drummed home into my head was that drinking alcohol is normal and there was something *wrong* with my dad. You've got to see what is wrong with that picture.

Alcohol is "normal" but what about when it goes wrong? Well, society doesn't leave room for that, does it? The message is taught to us that surely something must be wrong with *us* if we don't end up having a brilliant time or lead a phenomenal life with alcohol in it. At no point does anyone punt the facts. No one is making flashy adverts about the fact that alcohol is a poison and that it causes disease, ruins relationships, and makes us feel bad. Advertising those facts might cause liquor sales to drop and society can't have that!

 It's bizarre, but that's how the mind and society works. You can only break free from the shackles that are holding you firmly to alcoholism, when you start to *think* differently. If you put your mind to it and really start to think along the lines (and parallels) of alcohol being a bad friend; a backstabbing, toxic, evil genius, then chances are you might start the process of removing alcohol from your life. You might have the strength to remove your favorite drink from the pedestal you have had it sitting on for all of these years. Alcohol is a toxic friend. It seeks to take from you all that you have. And now it is time to fight back.

With this in mind, you might be able to see social occasions slightly differently. For Kev and me, our home was the usual spot to go for regular barbecues. We had (still do) a great outside entertainment area and a collection of music that's hard to beat. Being sober didn't mean that our social events suddenly dried up. It meant that I had to prepare myself for each event sufficiently. Just like anything new you learn in life, it's hard at first – but then it gets easier.

Prepping for Sober Socials

At first, my main concern was that I would have to remain sober in a space that I had become comfortable wine binging in. I was really worried that our usual crowd would come over and it would be utter torture for me. But you know what; it actually turned out okay. I think being in my own space actually made it a lot easier.

I put a lot of prep work in, when friends were coming over. I put a few inspirational sobriety and self -improvement quotes on post-it notes in places where only I would encounter them. They were stuck on the inside of the glasses cupboard door, back of the bathroom door, and in my jacket pocket (yip).

I made sure that I had plenty of sparkling water and non-alcoholic wine on hand. I also focused on ensuring that there was a lot of delectable food, so that I could spend my evening snacking instead of thinking about sipping.

When the time came, all I did was breathe through it. I told myself that everyone would be tipsy after the first hour and that I would be safe to relax thereafter and not feel so on edge. No one really pays as much attention to you as you think they do, when they are drinking. I actually found a certain power in being the only sober person in the room eventually. It can be empowering if you let go of the mindset that you are losing out. Don't go down the fear-of-missing-out road.

If you can, try to put the act of drinking out of your mind. What most of us do when we sober socialize is think about how sober we are, how much wine we aren't drinking, and how much fun everyone else seems to be having. It is actually this thought process and pre-occupation that is holding you back. When you are drinking, you probably aren't giving much thought to the act – you are on autopilot. Try to do the same when you socialize sober. Drinking is not the point – having fun is the point. For all of this time, you have thought that alcohol is the way to have fun, but in reality it is not!

Throw yourself into the conversations happening around you. Listen to what people are talking about and talk with them. Put all your focus on having those conversations. Ask questions, make comments, and offer opinions. You might just find the conversation fun or entertaining and you may have a few of your own stories to share. I certainly did. And when you start to think about the fact that you are sober or that everyone *seems* to be having more fun than you, bring your mind back to the conversation and the present moment. Just breathe through it. Talk more.

You will find that people love to talk about themselves, so you really just have to ask a few questions or make a few strategic comments to get someone talking (which takes the pressure of you). The rest of the hard work is done by *them,* not you! Of course you will have the urge now and then to grab a glass of wine and join in, but just resist. See how long you can resist. Make a point of talking yourself down from the ledge. Play it forward. Consider what will happen if you *do* drink. What will tomorrow be like? How will you personally feel about yourself tomorrow? Playing it forward has always helped for me. I try to imagine what could happen if I do have that drink. I think of all the ways in which I will suffer. I will have a hangover, I won't be able to do anything tomorrow, I will eat badly, and I will have wasted all the hard work I have done, for starters.

Once, I even recorded a video of myself on my mobile phone for *that* moment I am on the verge of having a drink. The video is me, telling me not to do it and why. Twice that video has helped me to turn around and say no. It might work for you.

Being able to socialize sober didn't happen instantly for me. It took practice for me to get through a social event sober, while feeling completely comfortable. If you put your mind to this process and use this technique and method of thinking as a guide, you will find that it gets a little easier every time.

What do you do when you aren't controlling the setting that you are socializing in? What if the gathering is happening at a restaurant, bar, or a friend's house? Then what? I usually apply the same logic and process. I set calendar reminders on my mobile phone with inspirational sobriety quotes and reminders of why I am choosing sobriety. I also play it forward every time I feel on the verge of having a drink. I think of how much I will regret drinking in just a few hours. This isn't a magic cure, but really can go a long way toward helping you to resist.

Make eating the main event for you at any gathering that is out in a public place. I remember many years ago, before I ever contemplated getting sober, seeing this strategy in action. There was a girl (who I only ever saw have 1 or 2 drinks max) who would join our group of friends for drinking sessions. Right splat bang in the middle of a drinking session, a big burger, bangers and mash, or a platter or two of bar snacks would arrive at the table. She would thoroughly enjoy her meal. If it was snacks, she would happily share them with others. I noticed that a lot of the people drinking would get hungry eyes and start ordering food of their own, which is great, because full tummies often lead to tiredness and early nights! I often fell victim to this ploy of hers, and I didn't even realize it. She had made her meal or snacks the highlight of her outing, whereas we had made drinking our highlight – and guess who felt a whole lot better waking up the next day!

CHALLENGE THE URGE TO DRINK

In the beginning, I did a *lot* of Google research on how to curb the urge to drink. On some level, I didn't want to drink, but on another level I wanted nothing more. I was pulling in two directions and that's when I came across the term of cognitive dissonance. Cognitive dissonance is when you want to stop doing something, but you do it anyway. It's when you don't quite believe in or agree with what you are doing, yet you keep doing it.

We put this down to cravings. It's the urge and temptation to drink that makes us abandon all the hard work we have done and reach for that bottle again. Keep in mind that an urge isn't one thing; it's a combination of things. It's the thoughts that creep up on you paired with the physical desire to drink to relax or improve your mood. It's the sensations and emotions that come with not having the drink. These could be frustration, irritation, and even anger. You might even feel a sense of desperation. An urge is a combination of these things and that's why they are so hard to beat. It's like you are being attacked on several fronts and you only have enough to defend one of those fronts. It feels as if the urge is going to beat that front and win. If feels like you may as well just have that drink. It's a bit defeatist but many of us do that.

The urge to drink will come. I remember when it came for me and I found myself behaving in a way I never thought I would.

A fine example would be a typical Friday evening, after a long week of work. I wanted nothing more than to escape my computer screen, to relax and have fun with Kev. For me, the only way that fun and relaxation could be achieved was with a glass of wine.

After I quit drinking, I knew I had made a commitment not to drink and so I felt miserable. I allowed myself to be so negatively affected by a decision I had made for myself that I remember allowing several weekends to pass by. Instead of actively enjoying them, I sulked; felt left out and had a general woe-is-me attitude.

I didn't want to do anything, because I was so depressed. I was upset and miserable because I *couldn't* drink. When I think back on those days I realize just how immature and unfair I was being on those around me. I realize that I was imposing it on Kev and he didn't deserve it. I also realize just how many great days I missed out on. I had slipped into a cycle of complaining about my life, while ignoring the possible solutions available to me. I wanted a better life, but I didn't want anything to change.

I was behaving like one of *those* people. We all know one of *those* people. The type of people that complain about the state of their lives or their weight or a problem they are dealing with, but fail to grab the opportunity to turn the situation around. It's like someone who is overweight and miserable about it, complaining every single day about just how overweight they are, and then going home to eat cake for dinner each night.

At first, we probably empathize with people like this and we offer advice, support and a few ideas of how to combat the problem. But then we notice that said person disregards the advice, refuses to try any of the ideas and options offered, and continues to live a lifestyle that causes or contributes to the very thing they are miserable about. We get vaguely annoyed, don't we? We start to lose faith in the legitimacy of that person's problems. We start to get a bit more hardline with them or we simply stop giving them the time of day.

Think about it. That's exactly what most of us do when it comes to alcohol. I personally hated the way my life was going. I hated the way arguments cropped up when I drank. I hated the hangovers. I hated the days filled with bad eating due to hangovers. I hated feeling tired and lethargic. I hated the work I missed. I hated the fact that my late-night drinking sessions made me lack the ambition I needed to start my own business for so many years.

I hated a lot of things about alcohol and I complained about these things often. I *knew* it was alcohol causing these feelings of hate. Only alcohol was giving me a hangover. Only alcohol was making me put on weight. Only alcohol was causing me to become tired and lethargic. Only alcohol was robbing me of my ambition and opportunities. But what did I do? I kept drinking. Is it enough to say that I kept drinking simply because I liked it? Did I keep drinking even though I was miserable, just because it was fun for a few hours?

It feels like I took far too long to decide to be a different kind of person. I wanted to be the type of person that eliminates negativity from my life and actively works at making positive changes. This took a lot of personal work. I had to be fully prepared to put in the effort to make positive changes in my life.

The only way we can better our lives is if we are willing to put in the work, take the steps, and make the change. No one is going to make our lives better for us. It is up to us.

Here's the good news.... Urges to drink or "party" are short-lived. If we take the time to monitor *when* we feel the urge to drink and *what* our possible triggers are, we can predict them and somewhat control them.

Let's take for instance; you notice that you have the urge to drink on a Sunday afternoon. This is typically the time when the sun is shining and you're sitting in the garden with your family, other half, or friends. Now we know something about your urges and their triggers. We know that warm sunny days and social gatherings are your triggers.

Does this mean you should never spend time in the sunshine with your family and friends if you wish to stay sober? No, it doesn't mean that at all. It just means you have to change the circumstances a bit. Perhaps get your Sunday sunshine, but make the occasion a bit more productive. The options are endless. You could plan a mini boot camp for you and the family in the garden and get a bit of a workout. Or you could play games like soccer, catchers, swing ball, softball or anything else that the whole family might like to get involved in. Perhaps you can do a bit of container gardening so that you get your sunshine fix without having time for a drink. Be prepared to change things up a bit. Think of it as refurbishing your habits.

On the social front, perhaps arrange to see your friends and family for a social at a time of the day where drinking isn't the norm for you. Head out to a sunny restaurant for breakfast – not exactly the type of meal that goes with a drink. Altering your behavior slightly can make the biggest difference.

In cognitive behavioral therapy, you can learn to change unhelpful thinking patterns and reactions. This means that you can actually work at changing how you think about alcohol and how you behave in situations where alcohol would usually be the main event. You can change how you react when you have the urge to drink. There's a theory out there that you can overcome the urges and change both behavior and reactions, if you recognize the triggers, avoid high-risk situations, and then have a coping strategy or mechanism in place. This theory is explored in more detail below.

RECOGNISING TRIGGERS

The urge to drink is sparked by something both within and without us. This means that it is about what we encounter and experience as well as what we think in our heads. An external trigger can be a number of things. It can be a person, a time of day, or even a place (you could drive past your favorite pub or restaurant perhaps and feel triggered).

External triggers can be easy to get a handle on, because you can predict them and apply avoidance tactics. It's the internal triggers that are often harder to get around. These aren't too predictable.

A trigger can present itself at the most unexpected time and that's what makes me want to damn them to hell! For me, the internal triggers made more sense after I took the time to monitor when I felt triggered. I had a mini notebook and pen in my handbag and when I suddenly felt like a drink, I wrote down a few things:

- What am I doing right now?

- Where am I?

- What time of day is it?

- How am I feeling?

- What am I thinking about/listening to/talking about?

I soon started noticing that I wanted to drink the most, when I felt happy or excited. Much the same, when I was bored, angry (just after an argument for example), or feeling low, I would want to drink. These are the times when I most wanted to binge drink.

As it turns out, my feelings and emotions are my biggest internal triggers. Not specific feelings and emotions. No, that would have been too easy. I find that I am triggered by any feeling or emotion that I have to deal with. I feel the urge to drink so that I don't have to deal with my feelings. Learning this was actually really valuable.

I think it's a good idea to track your triggers and urges for a few days or weeks. Write down when you feel the urge to drink. Make a note of what it feels like and why you think it has triggered you. This will help you to set a strategy in place to tackle the urge. If you know what the trigger is, you can avoid it. It's fairly simple.

Over the years I have learned the value of monitoring my triggers, understanding them, and then trying to eliminate them. On one particular occasion, I remember realizing that one of my triggers was a strange (or unexpected) one in deed.

It was a sunny summer Saturday afternoon and I was at least 4 months alcohol-free. I was going about my day as usual when Kev arrived home with the type of news I had come to dread.

"A couple of the guys from work and their wives (and kids) would like to have a few drinks in the park this afternoon".

Near our home there's a hiking area that has beautiful picnic spots. People are known to drink there in excess.

It's the kind of place people *want* to drink. The sun seems to set just right, the families kicking a ball around and laughing makes you feel at home, and before you know it you have downed a good few glasses of wine amid the good feelings and catch-up session.

I knew that I would be thrown into a group of people that I barely knew and they would be drinking. I was instantly on edge. I had my hackles up and was feeling triggered. That being said, that trigger is not the *actual* trigger I am referring to here.

After asking all the overly-insecure questions of "who will be there?" and "will we stay very long?" I decided I had to earn myself some partner points and put in the effort to go – for Kev. I was worried I was becoming a bit of a bore and a hermit since I quit drinking and I didn't want to become one of *those* partners that never attended work socials.

I was fully prepared for the occasion by the time we left. I was armed with fizzy water bottles, loaded up with bags of chips as snacks, and I had good old Fido tethered on his lead (having a dog on a leash is a great distraction for when you want to avoid humans in the park by the way). I was ready. I could do this.

The drive to the park was painful. I kept catching myself thinking "maybe one will help to take the edge off" and "it's been 4 months, one can't hurt". I was on the verge of being shaky about it all and I am pretty sure Kev noticed, because he kept giving me reassuring leg rubs and looking almost pitifully at me. I kept repeating to myself that I would be fine. It would be fine. It's only a few hours. And then, as if all too soon; we arrived and the moment I had been dreading was upon me.

We were setting up beach chairs on the grass and saying our hellos, fully expecting for drinks to be the very next point of conversation, but it didn't happen.

I quickly yanked my fizzy water out, poured it into my sippy cup and sat down. Phew. I had a drink in hand – surely no one will ask now. I am always awkward the moment I arrive at gatherings and events. It's weird. It's like it takes a few minutes for me to "warm up" and relax into it. Alcohol used to speed that part of the socializing experience up for me, but I no longer had that crutch and I was on edge. I find it hard to make conversation when I feel this way. I almost want to crawl into myself. It's not shyness. It's severe social awkwardness/anxiety. It's one of the reasons why I loved to drink so much in the first place. It would loosen me up and help me to avoid this very feeling.

As Kev delved into our bags and hauled out his beers, he turned to offer some to those around us. To my surprise, everyone except one of the other men in the group, turned him down. At first I got completely paranoid and thought Kev had told his work mates that I had a "problem" and as a result they felt pity for me and were avoiding drinking. I felt my cheeks flush, but luckily it passed when one of the ladies explained that as a group, they were doing a 2 week no-alcohol stint and so everyone was drinking alcohol-free beers and sodas.

And that, ladies and gents, was my strange trigger. I was suddenly in a group of sober people. My sobriety was being shone in an entirely new spotlight. I felt instantly awkward and wanted a glass of wine. Why? I think it had something to do with the fact that I knew everyone would spend the evening sober and that there would be more pressure on me as a result. I started to obsess about how they would take note of who I am, how awkward I get, and how little I seem to have to say when I am sober. I felt more on the spot in a group of sober people than I ever felt as the only sober person in a group of drunken people. I don't quite know how to explain it, but this particular trigger was excruciating.

This might sound outrageous to you. Maybe you dream of such social gatherings in your life. Maybe you love the idea of sitting sober, with a group of sober people, making conversation for 3 to 5 hours. I on the other hand had absolutely no coping mechanisms for this new situation I found myself in. I was only prepared for a scenario where I was the only one not drinking. I could apply all my strategies to get through the event, everyone would get drunk (except me) and then I would ease Kev in the direction of home, letting him believe it was his decision. What now? Now I actually had to have social skills, which is something I only ever got from alcohol.

The sneaky thing about sobriety is that you never know what you are going to be faced with and there's nothing you can "take" or "drink" to take the edge off, or make it seemingly easier. Who knew that socializing sober with other sober people would be one of my triggers – well, now you know; anything is possible and that's the true nature of triggers; they can be unpredictable.

AVOID HIGH-RISK SITUATIONS

If you know what your triggers are, you can try to set avoidance tactics in place. If you feel triggered when you are home alone, try to avoid being home alone. Visit a friend, invite the family over, or go shopping – don't be alone.

Another tactic is to avoid all types of high risk situations, at least for a while. This means that the chance of you being triggered is minimized for a time. In order for me to avoid high-risk situations, I make sure that I don't have any of my alcohol preferences in the house. Kev has his alcohol stash and luckily it's not what I like at all. If you share your home and there's alcohol in it, ask for it to be locked away or hidden from you.

In the beginning, if you feel social events will trigger you, don't go. It's as simple as that. You can only go to social gatherings where drinking will happen, when you are in a better position to say 'no'. Don't fret about turning down invitations. Remember that this doesn't have to be forever; you are just saying "not this time" for a while.

This doesn't mean that you have to cut ties with your friends. Instead, try to make alternative arrangements to see your friends. Invite your friends to a Saturday or Sunday morning breakfast or gather some friends for a Park Run event. Go to a flea market in the morning with your closest friends. Start re-arranging your social events, so that drinking is less likely to happen. Your social life doesn't have to vanish; it just has to change a little.

If you are going to attend social gatherings where there will be alcohol, you need to be firm with yourself and those around you. You see, there's direct social pressure and indirect social pressure to deal with.

Direct social pressure is the urge you feel to drink when the people around you are teasing you and pushing drinks on you. You know the usual "just have one" or "you are so boring nowadays", or when someone just offers you a drink and you're unprepared with a firm "no"? This is how direct social pressure works, as people are blatantly pressuring you.

Indirect social pressure is on you. This is when you feel triggered to drink just by being in the presence of other people in a social setting. You end up putting the pressure on yourself to drink, even if you aren't offered a drink. You might tell people you aren't keen for a drink and they respect your wishes and leave you be, but then you decide you will have more fun with a drink and so get one anyway. That is indirect social pressure.

The best thing to do is to set your mind firmly on the fact that you aren't going to drink. Already have your mind made up and go over what you will say (in your head) before you go. When someone offers you a drink, don't look conflicted and um and ah. Rather say firmly "not for me, thanks" or "I've already got one, thanks" and leave it at that. Don't wax lyrical about why you aren't drinking. You don't *need* to offer any explanations. Most people only leap into questioning if you look and sound like you are doing something (not drinking) that you don't want to. Don't hesitate with your response, make eye-contact and say "no thanks" without quibble. Be firm with yourself and others. "I am not drinking today". No negotiations.

STRATEGIZE FOR SUCCESS: COPING WITH TRIGGERS

Triggers are a reality. You might even do what you can to avoid high-risk situations and work through your internal triggers and still, you are faced with the overwhelming urge to drink. You might start to wonder if you are truly broken. You may ask yourself "What is wrong with me? Why can't I do this?"

I have asked myself these very questions many times. I have had these thoughts more times than I care to admit, to be honest. I couldn't understand what was wrong with me, especially in the beginning. I knew the evils of alcohol. I wanted it out of my life, yet something inside me still wanted it, craved it, and needed it.

It might be some comfort to know that no, you are not broken. Instead, your brain is just testing you. You brain needs a bit of time to learn a new way of thinking about alcohol. It also needs to prepare a new way of behaving when you have an urge. It's a lot of work for your brain, so give it the time it needs. You need to handle your triggers (firmly mind you) until your brain accepts that *this* is the new norm. And there will be a new norm – trust that.

If you read a lot of quit lit, you already know the science behind it. You know habits aren't formed overnight. It probably took you a few years to develop a drinking habit, so it's going to take a bit of time to get a new habit formed. You should find comfort in the fact that you *know* you can form a habit. You've done it before and you *can* do it again.

I learned a few effective urge-handling strategies while I was slogging my way through the first few months of sobriety. They came along in typical trial-and-error ways and with a bit of hard work, I finally found what works for me. When an urge sneaks its way into my head and I am doing all the usual bargaining of "but it's just a few drinks" or "I can moderate" or "I deserve to have fun, don't I?" – I just apply my strategies.

One of my strategies is to sit with the feelings. I observe them. This is actually something I learned through a mindfulness practice app. When the urge arrives, I ask myself questions about it. I ask how long I think the urge will last. Do urges last forever, or will it go away? I ask what will happen and how I will feel if I give in to the urge. I ask myself if it would be better to wait the 15 to 30 minutes for it to pass or to pick up a bottle and end up losing several hours of the day. Sitting with feelings like this really helps me to discredit the urges and thoughts.

Another good strategy I turn to is to get real and remind myself why I wanted to quit drinking in the first place. I had many days where I woke up so hungover that I couldn't function. I got into so many alcohol fueled fights with Kev, and the people in my life before him, that I am embarrassed. I have written a really long list of the reasons why I don't want alcohol in my life anymore, complete with a few reminders of the occasions when I truly embarrassed myself the most. My brutally honest list serves as a big wake-up call every time I read it. When I feel like drinking, I pull the list out and then I decide that if I no longer agree with the reasons why I shouldn't, then I can drink. As it turns out, I still feel that the reasons I wanted to quit in the first place are warranted and my mind set is snapped back into thinking about sobriety. It's not nice to remind yourself of the embarrassing and hurtful things that you did when drunk, but it really does work in deterring you from reaching for a drink.

In the beginning I tried to go it alone, but that didn't really work. Telling someone about my desire to quit drinking really worked for me. My sister was the person I confided in and we agreed that if I felt like I was going to drink, I had to phone her first to talk about it. This plan has actually brought us a lot closer. Now when I call her to tell her I have serious urges to drink, we end up talking and laughing for over an hour and by the time we hang up, I don't really feel like drinking anymore. One of my sober friends has a sober buddy and a sponsor. It's nice to have someone to call or message when you're on the verge of drinking. It's a great safety net and they can at least take a stab at talking you down.

Distraction became a fine art for me and it works wonderfully. When I forced myself into sobriety, I suddenly realized that I have other interests. The downside was that I lacked the drive to get involved or do the things I was interested in, because of my constant hangovers and planning around drinking. Now that I was sober, I still felt lethargic and disinterested, but only because I hadn't changed my routine. I decided it was time to make some changes!

Forcing myself to dabble in things I am interested in, is the best thing that I have ever done for myself. When I am feeling triggered, I grab my skipping rope and head outside for some jump rope, or I simply run on the spot. I have created a very upbeat playlist on YouTube for myself and when I start jumping around, running, or dancing manically, I actually lose track of time.

Of course, when I am done, I lie on the grass to catch my breath, have some water, and then I go for a long soak in the bath. It's a great distraction. When I am feeling too low to get active, I go straight to a bubble bath with some quit lit, or I Google a new recipe and whip something up. Find a few distractions that will work for you and write them down. Remember them when you feel like drinking. Haul the list out and see if there is anything on there that you could do right then and there that would get your mind off drinking.

I have found that challenging the urge I am faced with is a great strategy too. I ask myself "what the hell is this urge thinking?!" I now have a stance of not allowing an urge to enter my life and wreak havoc unchecked. Last time I checked, I was in control of my life, not some random urge. When the urge arrives, I stop what I'm doing and ask myself why. Why do I want to drink right then in that moment? I analyze the situation closely and pick it apart. I look for all possible reasons to discredit it. I get argumentative and right up in the face of that urge. Do I really *want* to drink? Will drinking really make things better? Why do I think it's a good idea to drink when I know that it's not? I have made a point of getting absolutely brutal with my urges. They never go easy on me, so I never go easy on them! I seek to make the urge feel unwarranted and insignificant. I tell myself that it's an urge, not an instruction and that's its completely unwelcome in my life.

I treat the urge like an unwanted intruder that's obnoxiously pushed its way into my circle of loved ones. I treat it like I would treat someone who seeks to harm those I love. I send it packing. I choose to put it in its place. This can result in me feeling angry and annoyed or frustrated. I have hung a boxing bag in the tree in the garden and I go out there and give it hell. If you go this route, learn to punch properly and get protective gloves (I learned the importance of this the hard way).

DRUNK CONVERSATIONS

Are drunk conversations really easier than
sober ones? Think about it? How awkward are
sober conversations? They probably aren't as
awkward as you think they are. You probably
don't realize this, but the majority of the
conversations you have had in your life, have
been sober. Unless you drink from morning
until night, that is. Throughout our childhood
we had conversations sober – were they
awkward? Are drunk conversations really
easier, or do we just *think* they are easier?

One of the biggest reasons I never wanted to
quit alcohol was because it seemed as if
conversations just flowed when I was drinking
(and when others were drinking with me). You
know, when you're drinking you can chat to
people for hours and hours. You can laugh,
joke, and feel at ease.

If you were sober, you probably wouldn't spend
nearly as much time talking to the same group
of people. For me, a typical weekend binge
would start around 4pm and end around 3am
the next day. That's 11 hours of drinking,
laughing, chatting and "having fun". Why can't
we do that sober? Is it possible to at least try
get to 11 hours of socializing while sober? This

is something I actually had a lot of interest in: the *why*.

I found it interesting to learn why we *think* we are great conversationalists when we are drunk. I gave it a lot of thought. What is different about *me* in a group conversation when I am drunk and when I am sober? Well, the clearest answer was that when I was sober, I would hold back a bit. I wouldn't blurt out my opinions and ideas without considering them first. I didn't want to upset or hurt anyone, so I would generally apply some tact first. This isn't a bad quality by the way, yet it's seen as a bad quality in a drinking situation. I also wouldn't get deeply into conversations about things I don't care too much about. I don't have an oversupply of confidence when I am sober – I care about what people think of me.

On the flip side, when I am in a group social and I am drunk, I just don't really care about what anyone thinks. I feel good, happy, and excitable and I say what comes to mind. I even get involved in conversations about things I have no interest in. For some reason my brain is interested in having an opinion about everything when I am drunk. My confidence is boosted and am I not held back. Instead, I readily get involved in activities and conversations.

This observation about myself helped me to better understand the findings I came across in my research. And I did a lot of research into why I have better conversations when I am drunk. I also wanted to know if I could change that and start to have better conversations while I am sober.

I did extensive reading on the relationship between alcohol and conversational skills and I found that the general idea is that we as a people (humans that is) *believe* that we are more fun and more sociable when we are drinking.

The power of the mind is very much at play here. I kind of know what this means. There have been several times in my life where I have arrived at a restaurant to meet friends for dinner and drinks, and felt quite drab right up until the moment the bottle of wine arrived at the table. In fact, I was probably quite fidgety until it arrived. The moment the wine bottle arrived, I would literally perk up and become happier and more animated – before even taking 1 sip.

Has that ever happened to you? If it has, what do you think that is?

It's your brain going "yippeeeeee! Now you are going to have more fun and be more sociable". If only we could get our brains to keep thinking that way without actually having a sip. Imagine you could just leave the bottle on the table and glance at it every now and then and you'd feel happy. Wouldn't that be great? If only we could be so lucky.

We know that the brain is already at play, sending messages of happiness, excitement and sociability the moment we *know* that we are going to have alcohol. The scene is set. We are already having fun in our minds before we begin.

The next thing that happens is that when you actually drink the alcohol, it does something to the amount of dopamine and serotonin released in the brain. It's a chemical reaction and your body is merely responding to the poison, but we like the way that feels.

When you swish that first and second sip down, the brain is signaled that alcohol is present and it raises your levels of GABA in the brain. Without getting too technical, GABA is a chemical messenger in the brain (it's a neurotransmitter) that sends a message to relax, reduce anxiety, and let go of the things that cause you stress. It's temporary; like wearing a mask to cover a scar. The stress and anxiety is still there, it's just masked. And guess what; it will still be there (probably worse) when the alcohol wears off and your GABA levels reduce.

GABA is a neurotransmitter that's described as "inhibitory". This means that the higher your brain's GABA levels are, the more your body temperature drops, your heart rate goes down, your blood pressure reduces and you *feel* more "loose" or "chilled". We're generally more open to conversation when we're feeling relaxed and aren't worrying about all the things happening in our lives (and each day).

When you continue drinking, your levels of dopamine are increased in the brain. Dopamine is responsible for sending those messages of pleasure in our bodies. Alcohol doesn't just make you feel pleasurable. It overstimulates the part of the brain that produces and releases dopamine. So, you're supping back on a drink and your dopamine levels are skyrocketing and it causes a high, buzzy feeling, which is what makes us want to drink. That buzzy feeling is somewhat exciting and makes us talk more doesn't it! What do you think happens next? You deplete your supplies and you suffer in the days to follow.

That's not all that alcohol is doing to your brain. It's also boosting the amount of norepinephrine in the brain. When norepinephrine is increased in the brain, you feel excited and happy and your inhibitions become lowered. This makes you more likely to act impulsively and lack the ability to truly consider the consequences of your actions. You might talk more openly, dance, shout, act the fool, laugh loudly and tell inappropriate stories – you might even take someone home with you. Yup, this has happened to me a lot. Remember that night I had Ray sleep over when Kev was away on a work contract... thanks norepinephrine!

It doesn't stop there though – don't worry, this alcohol and the brain section is almost over – it goes on only a little further! A few more sips of your drink and you can be sure that alcohol is further working its magic on the functionality of the prefrontal cortex of the brain. What's the prefrontal cortex? Well, it's a little part of the brain that helps us think clearly and rationally. We rely on this part of the brain to make decisions and think about issues and problems that concern us. Alcohol gets into the system and disables the prefrontal cortex to some degree. This means that its normal operations are disrupted and you can no longer activate *good* decision-making skills or rational thought process. This is why we speak more freely, laugh more openly, and act in ways we don't normally when we're sober. This proves something. It proves that you are not *you* when you drink. The alcohol has put to sleep the very part of your brain that makes you who you are. The part of you that decides what you think is okay and what you think is not okay. Now, anything goes!

While alcohol is wreaking havoc on the brain's behavioral inhibitory centers, information processing in the brain is slowed down immensely. Have you ever tried to talk to someone who is very drunk and seen that dead look in their eyes? You know that look like they cannot hear what you are saying and cannot comprehend the words coming out of you? They might respond in a totally unexpected way too. They might laugh or say something completely unrelated. This is because alcohol has deterred the brain from processing information and now it's unable to really think about what's happening.

The prefrontal cortex has quite a big responsibility beyond inhibiting certain behaviors like laughing loud or shouting our opinions out. It also is our inbuilt sense of control over our emotion-driven actions and behaviors. It's your prefrontal cortex that's responsible for willpower, that stops you from thinking and responding aggressively, and that keeps your emotions in check. When your prefrontal cortex is working unhindered, you might hear something that upsets you emotionally and makes you angry inside, but you are able to control yourself. When it's being deterred from doing its job by a drug (alcohol) it can't monitor those thoughts and feelings. When it is unable to do that, it can't provide you with that filter that stops you from shouting at your partner, crying in the middle of a party, throwing a bottle at another person, punching someone in the face, drunkenly breaking up with your kind and caring partner – you get the point. When you're drinking, your emotions are unfiltered and somewhat enhanced. An innocent comment might seem like a snide comment and cause a fight. A meaningless conversation could send you into a downward spiral of depression. That prefrontal cortex is important to us....debilitating it with alcohol is not healthy for our mental health at all.

Why are we better at making conversation when we are drunk? We aren't really. We just "don't care" about what we are doing, because our filter has been removed.

I found learning all of this information very helpful to my recovery, so I strongly recommend that you get onto Google and start researching the impact of alcohol on the brain, body, and our sociability.

HAVING EASIER CONVERSATIONS, SOBER

So, now we know why we feel we have better conversations and socialize better when we have alcohol in the picture. But how can we get this feeling and have the same fun and enjoyment talking with a group of people for *hours* without it?

Trust me; I have searched to the ends of Google for the answer to this one. The reality is that most people just don't want to chat to a group of people for 11 straight hours – it's not natural - but that doesn't mean that we can't put in a few good hours of sober socializing. It was hard for me in the beginning, I must admit. I find that I can usually join Kev and his friends at a drinking session for say 3 to 4 and half hours, before I want to head off and do something more productive (or relaxing) with my time.

For starters, I looked into how to naturally increase GABA in the brain. Armed with knowledge, I started putting in a bit of effort to do this, just before heading off to a social gathering. Going to meet a group of friends for a few hours in the afternoon? Get some GABA boosting in, in the morning before heading out. I learned a few GABA hacks along the way.

One particular GABA booster is Magnesium, so I got myself a supplement. It can help to regulate GABA activation across the majority of the brain and is involved in hundreds of biological processes.

Another good one for increasing GABA is yoga, as it increases GABA signaling. Meditation is also great and so is exercise. Going to spend time with a group of people and want to be in a good, talkative mood? Have a good yoga session or a hard workout before you go. The trick is to put your all into it. Don't go for a sedentary stroll before meeting up with a group of friends. Work out *hard*. It will give you a natural mood boost that's well worth it!

I learned that what I eat can also increase GABA in the brain. You cannot eat GABA as no food actually *includes* GABA. But what you eat can help the body increase GABA levels. GABA is produced in the brain from glutamic acid/glutamate, so you can eat to increase this in the body and therefore increase GABA levels in the brain. Here's what you can add to your diet.

- Vitamin B6

This is a required co-factor for GABA synthesis. Glutamate decarboxylase and B6 work together to catalyze glutamate in the production of GABA. You don't need to pop B6 pills (you can if you want) but you can have a healthy meal that includes B6 rich foods before you head out or while you are socializing (I love eating a meal while socializing these days). B6 rich foods include banana, broccoli, garlic, spinach, and Brussel sprouts.

- Glutamic Acid

You can also eat foods and drink beverages that have glutamic acid, which promotes GABA compounds such as Oolong teas, lentils, potatoes, tomatoes.

- Beneficial Bacteria

Most people don't know this, but GABA can also be synthetized in the gut by the presence of beneficial bacteria. How do you get beneficial bacteria into your gut? Fermented foods will do that for you. Snack on some foods that are rich in probiotics either before you head out or while you are socializing. Think of snacks like sauerkraut, fermented pickles, plain kefir. You can also take a multi-strain probiotic. It must be noted that studies have shown specific strains of bacteria including Lactobacillus Rhamnosus effectively boost the role of GABA in the brain. You should be able to find a probiotic at your local health store or online. If you want to do some interesting reading, use Google to research how gut bacteria can affect mood, cravings and so on.

I use these above methods to increase my own GABA levels and while I will never feel drunk-happy doing this, I do feel good enough get involved in a bit of chatting and laughing – I generally do have a good time.

- Caffeine/Stimulant

I must admit that because I don't drink any form of caffeine on a daily basis, when I go out to meet friends, I also have an energy drink or a cup or two of coffee, when I am out. It does elevate my mood a bit and is most helpful in keeping me in the moment (without getting tired or bored). This is as far as I have ever gone in terms of a stimulant. Yes, I had to quit caffeine in order to enjoy this benefit. Now I *only* ever drink caffeine when I go out.

THE "ME" COMPLEX

I cannot stress enough to you the importance of self-care when getting sober. I call self-care my "Me-Complex". On the morning of that fateful day I decided to quit drinking, I actually took a selfie. I don't know why, but I thought sending a picture of myself looking hungover and forlorn to my sister would inspire some sort of pity in her. I needed someone to see me as the victim I think, when in reality I was the monster. I still have that picture on my mobile phone and when I compare it to the way I look now, I admit that I am astounded. Drinking had been doing something to my physical appearance that should be considered criminal. I didn't notice it, but that's probably because alcohol shrouded my own eyes and vision from the truth.

When I think about it, I get a big and nasty flashback to one of our alcohol fueled fights many years back. I had been on a trip to visit Kev and we had jumped right into drinking the days away. There wasn't much time to spend on each other to be honest. I remember feeling particularly neglected because each night was a party and each morning was a hangover. Affection and love-making were at a bare minimum which was irking me even though I didn't have the energy for it myself. It seemed the constant cycle of drink, recover, repeat was dousing the flames of my sex drive...and seemingly Kev's too. As a binge-drinker I wanted it all though. I wanted the fairy tale relationship filled with magical nights, star gazing, cuddling, love-making, and languid afternoons, but I also wanted raucous laughing, dancing, stumbling around, and polishing off a few bottles of wine and shots of tequila every night. It just wasn't working out. It turns out, you can't have your cake and eat it, but my alcoholic mind was telling me I *could* have it all and that the reason it wasn't working out was *something else*. Never alcohol of course!

At the time, things were quite manic in terms of drinking and partying. With friends staying with us for a large portion of our visit, there was reason for a barbecue and a party every night. The first night was great fun. We drank up a storm, smoked a bit of weed, danced, and laughed the night away. The next day, the party continued, but the steam seemed to have dwindled. People were less energetic, we were drinking for the sake of drinking and while we stayed up until after midnight, it wasn't quite the party we expected. Exhausted we went to bed with no energy even for changing out of our clothes of that day. Waking up the next morning was something of a shock to the system. One of our friends had got the idea that a boozy breakfast was the way to make up for last night's lack of luster and so cans of beer were shoved into our hands and we were dragged outside into the sunshine. It must have been a beautiful morning, but sadly I didn't take much note of it. The idea was to drink until we dropped. There's something about next-day day-drinking. It's got all the potential of sparking a world war!

The music was blaring and we were lazing on the lawn, playing twister and loudly shouting nonsensical conversation at each other. I still have a few videos that someone took of us where you can see the obvious demise of my mood. I go from being somewhat chipper to looking sour and angry in the next video and in a third video you can see me curling my lip up and making obviously nasty comments to Kev. Yip, well, what did I expect right? Surely it was everyone's fault that I was in *this* state. I didn't quite fathom that the only person to blame for me reaching *this* state was me. I was the one picking up those drinks and supping them back. I was the one saying "more, more, more". I could have stopped, had a shower, eaten a meal, and just lazed in the sun at any time, but

I chose otherwise. I am not sure what quite turned my mood – possibly lack of sleep and irritation of constant visitors – but while everyone seemed jovial, there I was; moody, angry, and mean.

At some point in the afternoon, I completely lost my cool with Kev and others tried to intervene to "save" what was left of the day. It was already passed the point of no return and it was probably better left alone. But you know how those situations go. You're at a barbecue, two people get into an argument, and everyone wants to make it better by offering their advice, support, and obviously well-researched drunken counseling. And then it all came bubbling out. You know that alcohol sparks activity in the GABA receptors, right? It makes us drop those inhibitions. It makes us a bit more "loose" and fancy free. It makes your mind allow all of those unwarranted insecurities bubble to the surface, and worse than that; you're suddenly very vocal about them. It makes us say things we wouldn't normally say and do things we wouldn't normally do.

And that's what happened. I screamed at Kev "what the hell is wrong with you?! You barely even touch me these days!" Don't get any illusions of Kev being an angel or perfect gentleman in that moment though. He didn't hug me tight or reassure me like couples do in the movies – damn those fairy tales. Instead, he launched himself off the lawn and shot fiery mean words at me. Kev's GABA levels also seemed to be spiked as he wasn't holding back. The words seared through my very being and I will never forget them even though I understand that they were merely meant for impact. Drunken impact.

"Maybe if you put more effort into being pretty and attractive like you used to, I would".

The truth hurts. That's what they say right? I do remember putting in a lot more effort long before those words were ever uttered. Why had I stopped? I had more time and inclination for effort in the days before I started boozing hard. Night after night of drunkenness followed by long weekends that ended in Sundays that presented how-do-I-get-home problems, didn't leave much time for self-care. I considered it a victory that I managed to wake up and work in my PJs all of Monday!

I think deep down, I knew I looked a wreck. I had just been ignoring it for so long. My hair had some unsightly regrowth and hadn't had a trim or style in over a year, my legs weren't shaved all too often, my nails were never painted anymore, I had a puffy face and new wrinkles under my eyes that seemed intent on trapping every smear of yesterday's makeup, and my skin was spotty and oily (at nearly 40 years of age, that's not cool).

I was officially hurt.

I am not excusing Kev's harsh words or suggesting that my insecurity over how I look is something that should be shared by you, but here's a mind-blowing fact: alcohol makes us look like crap. Even if you are looking pretty good, you could actually look (and feel) a whole lot better. I look at my before picture and a photo I took at 6 months clean and I am floored at the difference. I never noticed a difference on a day to day basis when I looked in the mirror, but when I compare the two pictures; it looks like two totally different people.

Having a Me-Complex is really about sprucing up your look *for you*. It's a great thing to do when you're getting sober as the extra time makes it possible and you will really appreciate looking good and feeling good about yourself.

Alcohol makes us look like crap because it actually poisons us. Let's take the skin on your face for example. When we drink alcohol, it saps the amount of ADH (anti-diuretic hormone) in the body. This dehydrates the skin in a way that moisturizer just isn't going to help. This can leave your skin dry and blotchy or spur it into over-producing oil.

I used to get an incredibly puffy face after drinking. My eyes would be puffy underneath and my face would appear fatter. I hated it, but I chose to continue (madness, right?). The reason your face looks fatter and there's puffiness under your eyes, is because when your skin lacks hydration and vitamins (alcohol loves depleting vitamins) the skin begins to plump up/swell. When drinking, you are bound to over-exceed your sugar intake too, which leads to water retention, which in turn leads to a bloated face. I know this bloated face well. I have, often in the past, deleted photos on social media because my bloated face has been like a beacon in the crowd; embarrassing to say the least.

You might have noticed that I called my face a bloated beacon. Well, redness is something many of us are familiar with. My face would increase in redness with each drink and it would still have a bit of "bar burn" the next day. Not great for a day at work, I will tell you that! Alcohol increases blood flow, which causes dilation of the blood vessels in the face. Sounds fun, right? Luckily it's not permanent but some heavy long-term drinkers have been known to suffer lasting damage, so be careful!

The wrinkles; where did those come from? Well, they came from the consistent excessive drinking. At first, I assumed that it was from lack of sleep, but then I learned it's got more to do with the dehydration process and what alcohol does to your kidneys. When alcohol is working its magic in your brain and making you falsely believe you're having the *best* time, it's actually not being very kind to your kidneys. It's wreaking havoc with your anti-diuretic hormones, which sends your kidneys into overdrive, removing excess water from your body. It draws as much water as possible from your skin too, doubly fast. When this happens to the body and skin regularly, it can diminish your body's Vitamin A supplies. All of this can lead to premature aging and wrinkles.

If drinking a cup of tea did this to us, we probably wouldn't ever drink tea again. Think about that for a minute.

Then there's the extra weight we carry, when we drink regularly. I used to describe myself as skinny-fat. My arms and legs were skinny, but I had a bulge of fat formed on my belly. I hated it. I have always been slim, but when I hit my late 20's, I started forming a very stubborn muffin top. Even if I starved myself and just drank, that belly bulge was resilient. Thanks to alcohol that is! That extra fat around your waist is visceral fat which is actually quite bad for you. Studies have shown that visceral fat makes more of a particular protein type that inflames body tissues and organs. And that's not the worst of it. Visceral fat also narrows your blood vessels, causing increased blood pressure which as you know, is bad for your heart health. That little bulge we carry around our bellies; the bulge we jokingly call a "beer belly" or similar is not something to joke about at all. There's nothing cute about it when you realize that it's a big cause of serious illnesses, such as heart disease, Type 2 diabetes, stroke, high cholesterol, and Alzheimer's disease. These aren't things you really want to joke about, are they?

I have found reading up on the link between alcohol and diseases quite liberating. There's a saying that goes "knowledge is power" and that's ever so true. The more you educate yourself on the dangers of alcohol in your life (and on your body), the more your brain will start to see it as a threat. It's like finding out all the bad stuff about a partner. Like the perfect partner cheats on you and you suddenly find out. Suddenly the love affair is tarnished and most probably over, isn't it? It was just like that with me and alcohol. Cancer, heart disease and strokes are considered the norm in my family. Another norm just happens to be drinking. Do you think that is a coincidence?

Alcohol certainly caused me to carry around a bit of extra weight and that's not just because it increased my calorie intake. Alcohol deterred my body from its fat-burning functionality. That's very inconvenient in deed. When I was pouring alcohol down my throat, my body was putting all other functions aside (fat burning too) and focusing on breaking down the alcohol. This means that burning stored fat took a back seat and as a result, my belly bulge got a nice and steady foothold.

After Kev's crushing comment, I took it upon myself to be ultra-sensitive about my looks. I started to see myself through a critical eye. I developed an insecurity about how I looked all the time. It didn't matter how much sober Kev apologized or explained, the words were out there and I think the reason why I couldn't just brush them off was because I knew they were true. He might not have meant them, but that doesn't mean they weren't true words! I took a long hard look at myself. I was starting to look tired, dried out and almost faded if that makes sense. I was putting on stomach fat, sporting puffy eyes and a bloated face and my eyes were often yellow or slightly red. Not exactly a beauty queen!

When I decided to get sober, my appearance was the first improvement I noticed. And my insecurities about the way that I look were one of the first things that I worked on; with self-care.

Self-care is a very personal thing. You can practice self-care with a friend or partner, or go it alone. Either way, it's going to be beneficial to you. My first act of self-care was to incorporate more moisturizing bubbles bath in my routine. On Sundays, I have a standing date with myself in the late afternoon or evening. This was slightly strategic, as late afternoon and early evening is a trigger time for me, so it's good to be busy over that period. On self-care Sunday, I put a face mask on (usually ultra-moisturizing or exfoliating), I shave my legs, I run a bubble bath, and I have a really long soak. I drink sparkling water with lemon in it and I just *chill*. When I eventually emerge from the bath, I moisturize my entire body and then I remove last week's nail polish and apply something new. Something as simple as a fresh coat of nail polish for the week actually makes me feel so good.

Of course, the Me-Complex is about more than just shaving your legs and having a soak in the bath. It's also about how you choose to treat yourself on a daily basis. It is about making choices for yourself that promote your health and well-being and will ultimately impact on how you look on the outside as well as how you look on the inside.

An effective Me-Complex is about collaboration in multiple areas of your life. Make healthy food choices, drink enough water, get enough sleep, but more than that; make yourself feel good.

Get your hair done and keep it maintained (you should have more money for that now). Spruce up your wardrobe. Stretch every single day. Take your make up off at night. Go for a walk when you're feeling stressed. Have a cup of tea when you're feeling overwhelmed. Remove yourself from negative conversations. Distance yourself from people who are bad for you and your recovery. Go for a massage. Get away from devices for an evening. Book a ticket to a good movie or a show. Focus on becoming healthy mentally and physically, by doing things that are *good* for you.

Learn to put yourself first for a bit. You won't regret it.

~~No~~ Explanation Needed: Being Upfront

While I was drinking, and kicking up a storm of hangovers in my own life, I never really gave much thought to the reality that alcohol is a drug, just like every other drug out there. For some reason, because I imbibed, it was convenient to see it as otherwise.

I have never been to a barbecue and had to explain why I am not doing cocaine, meth or flakka, for instance. But it's quite different with alcohol, isn't it? If you announce that you won't be drinking, the comments will come flying, the questions, crinkled confused noses, and surprised expressions, will all be dished up for you on a silver platter of immediacy. In fact, some might even accuse you of being boring or old, before they have even experienced you sober. Alcohol is the only drug we have to explain not using and that's probably because the use of this particular drug is so widespread. It's built in (thanks media, thanks parents, and thanks society).

I remember one particular time in the early days of sobriety; I attended a book club in the late afternoon of a weekday. A friend of mine,

Mellenie, had been inviting me for months to join them. Her reasoning for me to go was A, it *actually* was a book club where the women discussed a book they had read and B, books are my *thing*. I love a good book – I still do. She always felt that joining her for book club would add some sort of value to my experience as a reader and of course, she probably wanted to get me out the house and mixing with other people. Mel had known for quite some time that I wasn't drinking and our friendship had progressed to doing non-drinking styled things; something I valued a great deal. I still value Mel's friendship. We have gone on 5k walks, been on breakfast meet ups, done morning movies, joined an art class together – as far as friends go, we were rocking it! For this very reason, my naivety led me to believe that book club with Mel would be a good idea.

I remember arriving, ringing the doorbell and being met by 3 women white knuckling red wine glasses (at 4pm mind you, but who am I to judge) and beaming from ear to ear while sing-songing at me "wine-o-clock". Oh no! I was *not* prepared for this. In the past I had been careful to always be in control of the situation, so as to avoid this very type of thing. I would bring my own alcohol-free drinks, I would come armed with reasons when people asked questions, and I would have a strong resolve already in set in place, so that I didn't cave. This time, I was standing there, feeling bare in front of these women. They had no idea that their happy demeanor and welcoming wine glasses were an agonizing kryptonite for me. I must have looked like a bunny in the headlights. Mel popped her head over too, showing off her purple-stained lips and teeth and appearing to be the happiest I had seen her in weeks.

I almost dropped my guard and agreed to a glass, just so I could get out of that moment, in which time seemed to be standing still. All eyes were on me expectantly "red or white?"

I tried to look busy in my handbag and appear unperturbed by what was happening around me. I nonchalantly replied "not now thanks, I am okay". I couldn't help but argue it out in my head. Why didn't I just tell them I don't drink? Now I am going to be faced with offers all night!

The reason I didn't tell them is simple and you are probably nodding your head in absolute understanding right now. I didn't want them, on first meeting, to already rule me out as boring. I didn't want these possible book-worm

buddies to lose interest in me, before I had
even had chance to offer my thoughts on the
book. I didn't want to be the old boring fart
that Mel invited out, because she potentially
felt pity for me. I wanted to be fun, I wanted to
be cool, and I wanted to be liked.

I believed that alcohol made me all of those
things.

The problem with my approach in this
situation is that it complicates things. It wasn't
even 15 minutes later when someone noticed I
wasn't gripping onto a glass of wine and soon
the offers came. It happened 15 minutes later
again. And then again and again, until I felt as
if my head might explode. And then Mel, who
had consumed more than her share of wine (or
so it appeared), blurted out "she can't, she's an
alcoholic!"

It wasn't Mel's fault. She was drunk. It was
mine for not being upfront. And there it was.
Someone had finally called me *that*. Up until
this point, I had only ever thought that word in
my head. I had never uttered the word next to
my name and everyone I'd dealt with had been
careful not to refer to me as one either. It
almost seemed momentous. *An alcoholic.* I

was the alcoholic; the only person in the room *not* drinking. The irony did not escape me.

I probably don't have to tell you how the rest of that evening went. The group went through phases of questioning me about that defining moment that I lost everything and had to go to rehab – apparently that is the only type of alcoholic they know of. They seemed almost disappointed at *my* reasons and story. Some looked awkward holding their drinks and others cracked horrible jokes. Needless to say; I didn't stick around too late that evening. After the book discussion was over, I ate a few snacks while chatting to Mel and then I snuck out, without drawing attention to myself. I must admit that I wasn't feeling all too spritely about things and felt as if I was missing out by going home. I wasn't going to let it ruin my entire day though. I stopped and got my favorite take-out on the drive home, I climbed into a hot bath with a Kindle book, Kev came home early after getting my brief message about the evening, and we ended up cuddling and watching Netflix movies in bed. It wasn't a bad way to salvage the evening and I actually got more value out of it. I certainly felt as if I had made the right decision when Mel sent me nonsensical messages early the next morning, claiming to be the host of a hangover sent straight from

Lucipher himself. I didn't see this as something I "missed out" on, but rather as a small victory.

In a way, I was lucky this was something that happened with strangers. I would have been far *more* mortified if this had happened in a room full of people I know. And that's when I told myself that being upfront is going to be a whole lot better for myself in the long run.

WHAT DOES BEING UPFRONT ENTAIL?

I didn't know what being upfront entailed at the beginning. I knew that I wanted to be more upfront so that the moment someone offered me a drink, the entire situation was shut down immediately. But I didn't know how to do that. Of course, I didn't want to go around attending events where I snapped at people or came across as rude or brash. I wanted to be gentle, kind, and firm. Almost an impossible mixture, but eventually I got it right. This is where you have to get creative. Everyone's life situation is different and so what works for one might not work for another.

For me, I decided to always have a few alcohol-free drinks stashed in a bag, in the trunk of my car. You never know when an unplanned situation is going to crop.

I made sure that I called or emailed all of the bars, pubs, and restaurants in the areas where I usually socialized. I made it my mission to find out precisely which of them offered a range of alcohol-free alternatives that are *always* stocked and available. This helps you to pick and choose which gatherings you will attend and recommend possible meet-up spots that suit *you*. An alcohol-free beer in a glass smells, tastes, and looks just like real beer, so I would order my drinks on my own tab at the bar (I would have a private chat with the barman/waiter about my requirements) and that would suffice for occasions where I really didn't want to get into telling people I don't drink, or when drinks were being pushed on me. I don't really do this anymore as my sobriety is not a secret to the people I choose to spend time with these days. That said, it's nice to know where you can enjoy a meal and an alcohol-free beer.

When attending barbecues and meet-ups, I would take my own alcohol-free drinks along. If someone offered me a drink, I had already practiced saying a hundred times before I arrived, "no thanks". No explanation. No "not right now" or "maybe later" – that leaves the door open. Just "no thanks". If the offer comes up again, I say "no thanks – not for me".

Be firm, don't hesitate and don't dither. You know you don't want it, so don't toy with the idea. Not for you or someone else. I find this works really well for me. I realized that when I seem confused or hesitant, it makes people question my resolve. When I am firm and decisive, they don't bother, because the decision has been made.

Outside Looking In

A feeling that I thought would never pass was that of being on the outside, looking in. I remember from the moment I announced to my "world" that "I don't drink", I was on the outside. I was on the outside looking in at all the fun I was no longer *allowed* to have. I was denounced. I took a rather ungraceful topple from my position of cool chick to boring old fart – in a heartbeat. And wow, did it hurt!

That's the thing about alcohol. It's almost like a cult (no I am not calling drinking a cult!). Those who are doing it are so dedicated and deeply ensconced in it that they refuse to see reason or even vaguely admit that alcohol is bad, unhealthy, toxic, and a drug. When and if, by some strike of good fortune, you manage to escape the grip of alcohol and get away, those who are left behind in the cult push you out, build a wall, and take stabs at you to keep you at bay. Alcohol keeps its chosen people close and those who have realized the truth about it are rejected, seen as having "something wrong" with them, and no longer part of the fun.

For a lot of people, "it's just no fun around sober people" – at least that's what they think. They know that a sober person isn't going to be as jolly or outgoing as someone who is drunk. As a result, someone who drinks would rather spend time with others who drink. It's natural, so don't take it too personally. In our "sober club", don't we find it better to be around sober people? We don't particularly want to spend our social hours around drunk people, just as much as drunk people don't want to spend their drunk hours around us. It's not just personal; it's deeply personal. It's personal on a level that not even drinkers understand. I took a long time to wrap my head around that one.

That's the thing about alcohol...it has such a hook in all of us. It's that toxic best friend that wants you all to itself (or its little group), and it makes you push away people that are different. It's a safety strategy to be surrounded by like-minded people. As the saying goes, "Birds of a feather flock together".

It took a while for me to realize that the sudden decline in social invites and text messaging about last weekend's happenings, were not because people suddenly didn't like me or have time for me; it was more because they weren't quite sure how to handle the situation themselves. And they weren't quite sure how to be around someone who doesn't drink, when they don't plan to stop or slow down themselves. When people aren't being overly obnoxious about your sobriety, they're being overly sensitive and confused about it – trust me on that one.

Tell people how to behave and tell people what you need.

I wasn't too far into my sobriety when I realized I would need to start telling people what I needed, wanted, and expected. I had no idea I had to do that until I did and you will be amazed at how much easier it can make things for you.

When I came out to my family and friends – when I told them that I was no longer going to drink - it was a big thing. In my mind, the moment I verbalized it to the people I loved, I was immediately accountable for my actions and that can be scary. Even if one of them offered me a drink and I decided to have it; I would be breaking some sort of vow in front of witnesses that were really important to me, simply because they *knew*. I knew it. I felt it deep within me. This was a deep plunge into the thick of sobriety. It was not something I could say one weekend and then revoke it a little further down the line. I couldn't suddenly decide that I got bored with it or have a hankering for a glass of my favorite red wine and throw all caution to the wind - ever. I did it though. It took the most part of a year to start outwardly admitting that I wasn't drinking. I stopped pretending, I stopped making up convenient excuses, so people wouldn't question me, and instead I owned it. I made myself accountable. It sounds terrifying and trust me, it was. It was terrifying to finally say that word "forever", but for me that was the only. In a way, it was terrifying and comforting to know that there was now an entire group of people who would look out for me, make sure I was okay, and hold me accountable if I seemed to be straying from the path.

Telling people what I needed and wanted from them was an important part of the process. I mean, when my sister asked me if it meant she couldn't have a glass of wine around me, when we went on our monthly girl's night, it was a valid question. It was also a valid question when a close ex work colleague, Anne, who I often had 'tequila night' with, asked me if it meant that I was no longer going to attend burger and beer night every fortnight. People just don't know what you need and what you want, in order to stick to your goals and be happy. And that can cause people to do things that might hurt you.

My sister might have spent the entire evening without a glass of wine, but been dying for me to leave just so she could open a bottle, guilt free. It would have really hurt me if Anne just stopped inviting me to burger and beer night and I realized she was still doing them with someone else. We open ourselves up to hurt by being vague, by pretending, by hiding what we actually want. Only we can decide what we want.

For me, I didn't want to be invited out to night clubs. There are those mystical sober creatures out there that can dance the night away entirely alcohol and drug free – it is safe to say that I am not one of those people. Besides, in the months that I had been working on my sobriety, I had realized that at my age, there was value and joy to be found in far more appropriate settings.

I wanted to be invited to burger and beer night, I wanted my sister to enjoy her wine with me around (she was always a '1 glass only' kind of red wine girl anyway), I wanted to be invited to barbecues and restaurants. I didn't want to be ousted because I was making a choice and changing what I *drink*.

I made sure that the people who mattered (those I was planning to spend my time with) were aware of the fact that I wanted the invitations to come and that sometimes I would just have to say no. Other times when I went, I wanted to drink my alcohol-free beer or wine without attention being brought to it. I wanted to be treated like I was me, not like some fragile flower that needed the truth hidden from her. Most of all, I wanted the people I care about to commit to at least a few sober socials with me. No, I wasn't insisting they come over to barbecue, without their beer or wine. I wasn't suggesting we head out for a girls night without the champagne. Instead, I asked if they would think about doing things like a Sunday morning breakfast at a sunny coffee shop, walking or running the Parkrun course with me on some Saturdays, going to a morning flea market, or pigging out on junk food and snacks at the movies one evening. This made me feel like my social life wasn't all about me trying to force myself just to get through a drinking occasion.

I am personally all for being practical. We can't give up a drug and expect to live our old lives/lifestyles exactly as they used to be. We have to be willing and ready to make some changes. It's a new start; why not begin by shuffling up that social life and having a new lifestyle too!

This really does bring me on to the final stage of this book. Don't worry though – there's still quite a way to go. I would like to talk about how I turned my sobriety into a lifestyle project and how somewhere along the way; I absolutely fell in love with my new self, and my new life!

Let's talk about what I call, "#Project Sober".

#Project Sober

One thing I noticed when I started out on this journey was that I got bored and frustrated with the process. Quitting alcohol is not like quitting sugar. The cravings are intense and it's hard to watch other people enjoying a social gathering - complete with alcohol - when you have to resist.

I started putting a lot of thought into how I can make my journey to sobriety more meaningful for me. I wanted it to stick this time. I wanted to be accountable and I wanted it to count. I also wanted my life to be fun. I had a preconceived misconception that being sober meant leading a mediocre life, sans enjoyment and sans fun. I was wrong.

I gave a lot of thought to what my sobriety was to me; what I *wanted* it to be. I decided it was going to be a project. It was/is a self-improvement project that isn't just about quitting alcohol, but also about becoming a better version of me and living my best life.

I don't just want to stop drinking. I actually want to deal with the reasons *why* I drink. I want to make the process so special and *fun* to me, that the thought of slipping up isn't something I easily toy with. I also want to make it special and memorable for those around me.

I made myself aware of the fact that while I was quitting first and foremost for me, I wasn't *just* quitting for me alone. I was quitting for all the people I impacted. My binge drinking wasn't just affecting me. It was hurting and confusing Kevin and making it hard for him to have a good and happy life. I was having a negative impact on those who I bumped into at bars and restaurants while intoxicated. I was having a negative impact on those around me every time I got loud and overbearing.

It's made Kev's parents worry about whether he is choosing the right soulmate and it's even affected my pets on the nights I have been too drunk to care for them both emotionally and physically. It's affected my friends who have been unable to dig beyond the surface and have a deeper conversation with me.

My binge drinking is far bigger than just me. And this realization made me cringe, when I finally came to it.

With all of this in mind, I came up with the idea of treating my sobriety like a self-improvement project. I made it a process of becoming a kinder, nicer, deeper, more likeable person, but not just on a surface level – on a *real* level. I made this round of sobriety matter to me and other people.

You're probably thinking that this sounds like a lot of waffle about nothing, but it's not. I believe that my self-improvement project is one of the biggest reasons I have made it thus far.

I didn't start big. I started with a simple list of things I would like to do in my life, or should do in my life, to inspire me to be better and to show other people how much it all means to me.

The list was also designed to help me become physically, mentally, and emotionally fit and healthy. I consistently update this list and it makes me feel really good. The list has hundreds of entries and I choose something from it as often as I can. I often repeat some of the tasks while doing a new one, as some are focused on health and fitness and that's a daily thing. Some are just really enjoyable or rewarding to do, and so they deserve a repeat.

Why did I do this? Mostly because sobriety without a distraction looks very boring and when you are bored, what do you want to do?

Drink. I wanted to make my sobriety so much fun that the prospect of drinking simply shriveled in comparison. And that's exactly what I did.

Here's a look at what that project task list looked like for me (and still does by the way). This is not an exhaustive list like my personal one, but it provides an excellent starting point if you want to #Project Sober your life. Why don't you make a list of your own or take a stab at mine!

- **Impulsive exercise.**

Today, select a random time, set the alarm for 10 minutes and spend the entire 10 minutes doing on-the-sport physical exercise. It doesn't matter what it is, just move around. Get moving! I have the luxury of working from my own home office, so on the days that I select this task for myself, I set 3 to 4 separate alarms to go off at random times in the day. When the alarm sounds, I jump out my seat and dance, squat, do jumping jacks – I just get moving. This is the very thing that actually got me *wanting* to listen to music and just dance for the sheer enjoyment again.

- **Add meaning to someone's day.**

During the struggle to get sober, a lot of us (that's ME) get so wrapped up in ourselves that we forget that *other people* have bad days too. Other people have worries and stresses and things on their minds. Just for today, give someone else the spotlight of your concern and care. Tell someone how much they mean to you and how much you appreciate the little things they do. Telling someone how you feel about them will actually make *you* feel great too. You don't have to fawn all over someone and get them wondering what's up, but a "hey you, you make my day" to your husband/wife or a quick "I just saw your social media post and must say that you are looking incredible" to your sister could make the world of difference to your marriage, your friendship, your relationship. It's all in the little things.

- **Overhaul something.**

Don't underestimate the power of pouring your heart and soul into something creative, even if you aren't particularly artistic. Making something or sprucing up something *yourself* can really inspire a sense of accomplishment inside you! It's also while doing something like this that you can get your mind off drinking.

For this one, I decided to makeover my home office. This is where I spend every day designing websites and graphics, yet for years now the walls have remained bland and there's nothing about the room that really screams "this is Jen's place". This seemed like a worthy project and I must point out that it is a time-consuming project. It took me at least a week of planning before I could even get started.

First, I took to Pinterest. I must tell you, I am a bit of a Pinterest addict. If there is any room in the house, the garden, or even a piece of furniture that you want to make better, Pinterest will provide you with endless images of inspiration. I think I have lost weeks of my life browsing Pinterest! Needless to say, I spent hours on Pinterest looking for make-over ideas for home studies and then I set out gathering what I needed.

Your next thought is probably about the cost. I didn't need to spend a lot of money at all, because I was not dead set on buying all new items for this project. I asked family and friends if they were getting rid of any old chairs (I got a nice one from my sister), paint brushes, wall papers, sand paper and other bits and bobs. In the end, I got everything second hand from people I knew. The only thing I bought new was the red paint that I painted onto the chosen "feature wall" and a bit of wall paper that's above my desk in a frame.

With my ear phones in, I set to work with my favorite playlist blaring into my head. It took me 3 weekends to complete, but it looks brilliant, even if I do say so myself. I get an immense sense of satisfaction as I nestle into the comfy chair that I sanded, painted, and upholstered *myself*, to read a book while waiting for Kev to get home in the evening. It's placed comfortably in my refurbished office space and the fact that I made it so beautiful really makes me feel good about it. Also, as a result of my focus on this, for 3 weekends I had little chance of drinking – I was too busy – I was too obsessed! Kev maintains that it is currently the best room in the house. Maybe I will tackle the other rooms when I get the urge!

- **Go on a physical adventure!**

If you are setting off on a journey to sobriety you might think that you have enough "adventure" in your life already, but so many people who quit drinking suddenly start to experience feelings of boredom. If you quit drinking, but simply allow the rest of your daily routine to kick in as usual, beware, because that's when the doldrums can set in. That's what happened to me. I started to feel like my life lacked "something". It felt like everything was boring and then suddenly I began feeling lazy and sluggish too. I would feel like life was boring and there was nothing to do, and on top of that, I was too sluggish and lazy to *want* to do anything. This is a dangerous grey area in sobriety I found. I suggest you do everything you can to stay away from this stage. I found that the only way, is to keep busy!

For a physical adventure, I really put my thinking box on and I came up with some good ideas. I set an "adventure day" for us, once a month. And boy, did I stick to it – even if Kev had a hangover! Lucky for me, Kev is always keen to adventure and he is the type of guy that doesn't often let a hangover get in the way of his commitments (especially if he has promised to do something with/for someone).

I used Google (thanks Google!) and found all the walks/hikes/nature reserves and parks that allow dogs in our area. Of course, we had to take Fido along, as I found it would give us joint focus and also limit the possibility of ducking into a restaurant or bar on the way there, or home. Once a month we would select a weekend that worked for both of us, to head out somewhere completely new. We would pack a picnic, load up Fido and head out. We still do this once a month, by the way, as it's a great way to spend quality time together, without the pressure of a crowded bar or restaurant.

When I plan the adventures, I personally prefer to choose the longer and more grueling hikes and walks, as they physically tire me out – for me, this is key! 3 to 4 hours of hiking, a delicious picnic, plenty of water-drinking and a longish drive back home...and that's me done! A lot of the hikes and interesting places we go to are about an hour's drive from home, so it's a nice road trip, which tends to take up some of the free time. Take your favorite playlist along, talk, sing, and dance in the car. Make it something worth remembering.

After a long hike or a tiring walk/run, I am keen to get home, bubble bath, put PJs on and watch a movie on the couch. I found that it really helped to physically tire myself out during the day on a weekend, as it made it easier for me to *want* to chill on the couch, watch movies, bubble bath and eat take out in the evening (night times are big trigger times for me). Sometimes I would read for hours in the bath after an adventure, feeling absolutely and utterly relaxed and at ease.

The only rule that I have for these trips is that we don't take *any* alcoholic beverages along (not even for Kev). This is *our* time and alcohol is not invited. Kev was happy to agree to this as I don't stop him from having a beer when we get home. If he feels like it nowadays, he sips on his beers when we get home. I busy myself feeding Fido, having a long bubble bath, shaving my legs, and reading a chapter or 2 of my book. If he wants to go meet the guys for a beer, I let him while I do my thing, maybe watch a movie, or order a pizza in. He appreciates the freedom to do so and it takes a lot of the pressure off me.

- **Go on *non-physical* adventures.**

What if going on a hike, walk or run, just isn't for you? What if you don't have a sporty bone in your body and the suggestion to get active has you rolling your eyes? I have heard from a lot of newbies in the alcohol-free world that they just aren't into physical activity. Some people don't dream of leaping out of bed and heading out on an adventure that requires running, climbing, sweating, or being out in the elements for long periods of times. That's absolutely fine – you are allowed to be *you*.

But that's were non-physical adventures come in. I am personally one for physical activity, but during the winter or colder weekends, going on a hike or running a few laps in the park are the furthest thing from my mind – so I fully understand! Lacking the desire to get physically active doesn't mean that you don't get to go on adventures. You just need get a bit more creative with the type of adventures you go on.

For me it was about doing something out of the norm – you know, getting away from the things that usually make me want to drink. And also providing myself with something new, so that I don't lapse into that "I'm bored and want to drink" vibe. Because we aim to go on an adventure once a month, I can plan ahead, which is great.

Not everyone has the budget to go away, but one weekend that's exactly what we did. We chose somewhere that had mountains, fireplaces and beautiful views. We didn't go far at all. In fact, you might find cool places to escape to that aren't hours away.
We had no intention of going on the long hikes

or running along the trail paths as it was the middle of winter. Instead, we decided that we would immediately ask for a list of activities and entertainment/recreation activities available at the reception desk when we arrived. If you like to get away, you will know that some hotels or hideaways have giant chess games outside, bowling allies, pool tables, indoor tennis courts, heated swimming pools, ping-pong tables, kid's arcade machines, and more. We decided that during our chilly stay, we would spend the day-time hours trying to do as many of the activities as possible. We checked them off the list as we went. It really did feel like we were kids again and to be honest, we had a blast battling it out on the foosball table and playing "killer" darts games. In the evenings, we ate as much as we could in the restaurant and headed to our accommodation to sit by the fire and enjoy mugs of hot chocolate and marshmallows. It was great!

If you are on a tight budget or want to do something closer to home, you could try a flea market. We have often headed to Saturday and Sunday morning flea markets, where we stroll around for hours with takeaway coffee or hot chocolate in hand. When we have seen it all, we head to a quaint coffee shop or restaurant for a full on breakfast. This is most often followed by heading to the cinema to watch a movie and then indulge in a coffee and sinfully delicious cake before heading home. You could browse a museum or stroll through an aquarium together! Even if museums don't seem to be the type of thing that interests you; just do it! You might be surprised at just how much you enjoy doing something different. As you can see, these are simple and small adventures, but so much fun. We often found ourselves heading out for evenings of bowling or indoor rock climbing, and we even once attended a cooking class, which was packed with fun and laughter.

- **Write someone a letter/postcard.**

I must admit that I have done this over and over as it's a fun and creative way to show someone that you care. I put a lot of effort into writing a message that will make someone laugh or smile, or simply feel good. I absolutely love hearing the happiness and excitement in the voices of those I send these out to. There's a pretty nifty app called My Postcard App (you can probably find it in your mobile phone's App Store) that I use personally. I am sure there are plenty of them. This type of app allows you to use your own pictures to send people postcards anywhere in the world. For me, it's a Godsend because my sisters all live in foreign countries, so I get to send them fun postcards from the comfort of my home. For me, this is highly valuable. I lost touch with my sisters for quite some time because of the way alcohol ruled my life, but now I get to reach out and show them that I care and that I am here.

- **Buy a journal and write about your feelings.**

You have probably read that a lot of people journal while trying to get sober. This was actually the very first task I selected from the list and it stuck. I actually write in my sobriety journal several times a week. My journal is something special. It's got musical instruments engraved all over the hard wood cover and a thick red strap that secures it. Within that book lies some of my happiest as well as some of my deepest and darkest thoughts and ramblings. I write when I feel good about my sobriety, because it's good to remember how good it can be. I write when I feel absolutely awful, so that there is an out for my feelings. I write when I am upset, angry, and confused. I have even written letters to the people in my life in there saying all the things I may never have the heart or inclination to say out loud. I feel it is important to get your thoughts, feelings, and troubles down on paper. This makes them a little more real and you can deal with them more readily. Writing your feelings down validates them. It provides a basis for you to start working through them. Until you have said them aloud (or the equivalent would be writing them down), you don't really have somewhere to start, do you?

- **Buy and read quit lit. Buy and read more quit lit. Repeat.**

For those who might not have stumbled across the term yet, "quit lit" is the term given to books that focus on sobriety. When it comes to reading quit lit, I love memoirs and personal accounts the most. If there's a quit lit book out there that can make me laugh a little, I am hooked. Remember that laughing is important too, so read books that lift the mood. You don't want to spend your entire journey dwelling on the negatives of drinking and never looking to the fun, positive life that awaits you.

I have bought many quit lit books over the years and strongly recommend that you do the same. I wish I knew about quit lit the day that I decided to stop drinking. I only cottoned onto it later, but it has still had a massive impact on my staying power on this "course". I have been sober for several years now and I *still* buy and consume quit lit as much as I can – I get everything on Amazon either in Kindle or paperback format. Audio books were never for me, because I find that the main message behind a book really sticks with me more if I put in the physical effort of reading it – but I know this isn't the case with everyone. My day 1 was *years* ago, but I recently just bought 2 new quit lit books. The thing is, you are never sober enough to stop reading quit lit. You are never sober enough to let your brain stray from the I-don't-and-won't-drink mindset. You need to keep reminding yourself of the stories, the reasons, and the risks. It's one of the most effective ways for me to keep sober. Some quit lit books might not seem for you, but once you start; finish reading them. There is always something to take away from each and every book. Within those pages are the heartfelt tale of someone's struggles and success. And the person who wrote it wants you to benefit from sobriety as much as they have.

I try to read a little of my quit lit book every night to get my mind ready for sleep and thinking about quitting, but that's not all. When Kev has friends over for drinks, my quit lit books really get me through it. On these occasions, I put in some effort to socialize to some degree, but invariably at some point of the evening I lose interest. This is usually about the time the drinks are flowing faster, people are repeating themselves, the music volume is increasing, and nonsensical laughter is filling our living room. I usually sneak off without saying anything, but if anyone catches me in the act, I quickly quip that I have a bit of work to finish up for tomorrow (the joys of working from home) and I make a quick escape. I head to the comfy confines of my bubble bath with a cup of tea and a good book. I find myself buying quit lit books as part of my milestone celebrations too – in fact, Kev has bought me quite a few of them.

- **Get creative (you don't have to be creative to get creative).**

Did you know that you don't actually have to be creative or artistic to actually derive joy and benefit out of art, or getting crafty? When I quit booze, I hadn't done anything artistic in many years, but there were some evenings where I just wanted to do something, other than watch TV. Getting creative is a great way to start forming new neural pathways in the brain. It gets your mind off the thing it's usually on (drinking) and it sets it on what you are doing right now. Getting creative is the ultimate distraction. Here's a few ways in which I got arty, crafty and creative.

> Paint by numbers.

I know, I know, this sounds like something for kids, but it's not really. If you take a look on Amazon, you will find several types of "paint by numbers" art packs available that are designed for adults. I have completed a gorgeous painting of a field of sunflowers and another one of wild animals. They came out so good (and I can't paint or draw to save my life) that we have them hanging in our home. Paint by numbers kits for adults will give you everything you need from the paint, the paper, the reference image, the brush. All you have to do is find a comfy spot and get painting. It's really therapeutic. If you have kids, get them kids paint by numbers sets, so they can do it with you.

> Beading (for jewelry) or décor.

Again, Amazon really saved the day for me here. I searched for adult beading jewelry making kits and bought myself a few of them. I have made several bangles, necklaces and even dream catchers using the kits I have bought. I sold several of them at a flea market once or twice, but mostly I use them as personalized gifts, or to donate them to charitable organizations, so that they can sell them for a profit.

> ➢ Scrapbooking.

This is something that I was obsessed with. When I had insomnia, I would scrap book. You can buy scrapbooking kits online and create scrap books that are themed (say for each holiday you have been on or for each person in your family). I have spent hours trimming photos and gluing pretty bits and bobs to pages. It's actually quite addictive. I am glad that I learned this particular skill as last year for Christmas, I gave Kev's mom a hand-made scrap book of her and the kids going through the ages, from little sprogs to current times. She loved the personal element of the gift so much that she cried as she paged through it. Scrapbooking is a great way to create meaningful gifts for the people you love and keep yourself busy at the same time.

- **Be a tourist in your own home town.**

I must admit that when I wrote this one down on my list, I wasn't sure where I was going with it. In the end I *thoroughly* enjoyed this task. Kev joined me with this one, which just added to the value I got out of it. By the time I quit drinking, it was safe to say that we had spent so many Saturdays and Sundays, either drinking or recovering from drinking, that going out and doing something else almost felt like a foreign concept.

To do this particular task, we went onto our local town's tourism website and of course, trawled Facebook and Google for ideas too. We wanted to see what tourists were doing in our area. We wanted to know what "things to do" and "places to see" came up in an online search in our town/city. And then, we made a list of all the things that seemed interesting or fun and planned to do them ourselves. Everything about this is fun, even the planning part. If your partner doesn't want to join you (or you don't have a partner), go alone or invite a family member or friend to join you. Kev and I usually do this together, but once we took his parents along and it was a great day out. One thing to remember is to be a tourist –

document it! Grab your mobile phone, take photos, and post memories on your social media platforms. You will love looking back on them one day, just like I do.

Not many people think about being a tourist in their own home town or area. Trust me, once you have tried it, you will be hooked. As residents of our own towns and cities, we become complacent in the fact that it's "home". We forget that there are reasons why people visit the very towns and cities we live in – because there's history, culture, and things to do and see. There are museums, lookout points, historical monuments, zoos, parks, aquariums, amusement parks, trails, and so much more!

For me, it became perfectly acceptable to laze around on a Friday night watching television, because I knew Saturday would feature a fun outing and I wanted to be fresh for that. Drinking would only ruin that.

- **Get Hooked on *Some* Form of Exercise – Make it Your Thing!**

You probably want to groan and roll your eyes. I actually chose this task within the first week and have been running with it since. Every day I wake up at 5.30am and do my morning workout. At first, I couldn't do much. I felt useless, out of breath, tired, and just not into it. But I found that the more I did it, the more I liked it. I am not one for Yoga or similar exercises, so I downloaded an app called Female Home Workouts (there's one for men too I believe). It basically sets a 15 to 20 minute workout for you to do every day of the week. You can do the exercises in a small space and it's a great way to help your body heal. Now, if I miss my morning workout for some reason, I get grumpy! I have to do it! If you don't feel like doing this, think about forcing yourself to. Just a few minutes a day is a good start. If the evenings are trigger times for you as they are for me, I strongly recommend that you aim to do a home workout every evening over that particular time period. I find it really helps to put those urges to bed!

Consider jump rope if regular exercise options don't tickle your fancy. I got hooked on jump rope fairly quickly when I started. I found inspiration on YouTube, because I love watching workout videos. One particular afternoon, I had some free time and I wanted to find a Pilates video. I hear it's good for muscle toning. It sounded like a good idea to have toned muscles, so I started searching for videos. During my search, I came across a great video showing a couple working out together, with jump ropes. The music was upbeat, they looked super fit, and the way they were moving was both impressive and beautiful. I was mesmerized – and so my jump rope addiction was born.

After that, I spent several hours with my eyes glued to YouTube videos. I found beginners jump rope videos; I watched choreographed jump rope dance videos, I couldn't stop. The next step was to buy a jump rope (thanks Amazon!). When it arrived, I remember snatching it out of the packaging, popping the YouTube video on and trying it out. I was terrible at it. The rope kept catching on my feet after a few hops, I got tired after about a minute and the running on the spot jump move seemed impossible. I didn't give up though. I kept practicing; I kept watching the videos and kept at it. I was jumping every day, soon every evening too. It's safe to say that I got quite addicted to jump rope. I stopped thinking about drinking when I was jumping. The trick is to choose a playlist that makes you want to dance. I still do jump rope for a bit every single day!

- **Grow something – nurture it and love it.**

This recommendation actually comes straight from the lips of my therapist, so you can go ahead and thank *her* for it! She felt I needed to experience the act of nurturing and caring for something, not because I had never done this before, but more because I felt broken and vulnerable – I was dwelling on it. The act of growing and nurturing something really impacted me. At first, I tried to grow an avocado pip. Where I live, this is no easy task. The pip alone took weeks and weeks to show any sign of life, but when it did, I cannot explain to you the excitement I felt. And, wow, the joy that little plant has brought me over the years. It is a well-documented avocado tree, I will tell you that! I strongly recommend looking into container gardening, hydroponic gardening, or if you have a garden and some free space – an actual veggie and herb patch. It can help to pass the time tending to the plants and it's a truly rewarding project. It's also great to while away the hours on the weekend in a sunny patch of the garden or on a weekday when I happen to have a few hours free. We now regularly eat our own tomatoes, lettuce, potatoes, and herbs. In the past, people used to gift me bottles of red wine for special occasions.

Nowadays, anyone close to me knows that some seeds or pretty pots for plants are far better gifts for me. You don't have to spend a lot of money to start growing some herbs, veggies, or flowers. In fact, it's more fun if you scoop the seeds out of the veggies that you buy and grow those – that's truly sustainable. That's how I got my tomato patch going.

- **Make a list of the reasons why you want/need to quit alcohol.**

When you write a list of the reasons why you no longer want alcohol in your life, it validates those reasons. This is a great way to deliver the message to your brain. Keep telling it that you want to quit and why. Once you have created the list, take the time to write a "goodbye" letter to alcohol. Touch on the reasons you mentioned in your list. Whenever you feel tempted to drink, get your list and read through the list of reasons why you *don't* want to drink. It might be just the resolve kick-start that you need.

- **Create an urge-buster.**

This is something that I did very early on in my sobriety. Someone once told me that I cannot simply wait to be successful at something; I had to strategize for success. I took this to heart and decided to write down a list of things I had to do in the moment, when I felt like the urge to drink. After working the strategy, I very often didn't want a drink at all. Make your own list, but mine consisted of: "do 1500 steps (calculated by my mobile phone's health app), drink 3 big glasses of water in a row, eat something, YouTube search standup comedy and watch at least 10 to 15 minutes, call your sister and ask about the kids." When I felt the overwhelming desire to drink, this is what I did. And it actually worked, as it passed just enough time for the urge to pass.

- **Video call someone you love**.

For me, this was my older sister, Jo. For the longest time I let my relationship with Jo fall by the wayside and when I got sober, I realized that I wasn't being a very good sister. I *never* actually saw or spoke to Jo for many months. It was like one day I just forgot all about her and that was that. When I got sober, I decided to change that. The first video call was awkward and uncomfortable (for both of us I think) but after a few, they became easier. I now call my sister once a week and I am glad that I decided to start doing this, as some of the conversations we have truly hold value in my life.

- **Make a photo wall.**

I must confess! I wanted to make a feature photo wall in my home from the day I moved in. The only problem was that weekends were the only days I wasn't working and unfortunately, I was always too drunk and hungover to ever make it happen. Because of this, I decided that making a photo wall had to feature rather prominently on my #project sober task list. I cannot tell you how much I enjoyed this one and how much joy this wall brings into my life.

I selected a wall in our living room that is adjacent to the television (you can't compete with the TV after all). Before it became our photo wall, it was merely a blank wall. It was nothing really to comment on. My next step was to pay a visit to one of my favorite sites; Pinterest. I researched photo feature walls and came up with literally thousands of ideas. I spent time witling down the options and then I spent hours poring over old memories and selecting photos to print. I spent even longer choosing photo frames mind you. I found an interesting project on Pinterest that teaches you how to make your own photo frames from things like old boxes, pieces of wood, and paper Mache – so I made a few of my own frames too! On my wall, none of the frames match and I love that. I painted the wall another color – it's now a feature wall that really pops in a deep dark purple! Once all the pictures were framed and the wall painted, I spent a bit more time arranging the pictures into the funkiest pattern and layout. I left a few spots open so that I can add a few new memories to the wall now and then as we go. I like this sober project task so much that I have already started doing the same thing in the hallway. Next up, the rest of the house!

- **Show interest in and promote someone else's cause.**

This is a selfless act to benefit someone else. Most of us know someone who has their own home business or sells a craft. Perhaps someone you know is raising funds for a good cause or trying to create awareness around a particular problem, topic or industry. Why don't you help them along the way by showing an interest in it? You can set about sharing the details on your social media, WhatsApp groups and more. It doesn't have to be *your* passion, but you can carry out an act of true friendship by showing support and promoting the business/idea/cause.

- **Spoil yourself properly.**

How often do you really spoil yourself? Most people would see their glass of wine after a long day as a spoil or reward, but what do you do now that it is no longer an option? When I first quit, I found that I was saving quite a bit of money. I am not the type of girl that heads to the nail bar or salon every few weeks for a spruce up – not at all. It wasn't just because I never had enough money for it. It's just I never felt like I belong in those salons. I handled everything *in-house*. That's changed and I am glad for it. At the risk of sounding utterly selfish, I must admit that I have chosen the task of spoiling myself a few times along the way.

I once had gel nails done – mani and pedi. On another occasion I went for a back and neck massage, as well as a facial. The one I loved the most was getting my hair cut into a new style that suited my new attitude. On the same day, I changed my hair color quite dramatically too. You won't believe how good this type of simple spoil can make you feel. When you are feeling fresh, bold, and beautiful, you won't want to

ruin it by pouring poison inside you. You will
also feel confident and bold at those social
events you have to navigate sober. I must say
that I feel more confident saying "no" when the
drinking peer pressure starts, if I am feeling
good about myself.

- **Bake someone a treat and deliver
  it to them.**

When I created this list, I put this particular
task on it, because I love getting baked goods as
gifts. What could be better than slogging away
at work and suddenly a batch of freshly baked
muffins is delivered to your desk with some
creamy butter and sweet jam too? Nothing can
beat that, trust me! I loved doing this, mostly
because I am not very good at baking and
wanted to get better, but also because people
loved their surprise treats (or at least they were
good at pretending they did!). Delivering a
baked treat to a friend or acquaintance also
leads to coffee and tea with a taste of said
treats. Delivery visits were always quick ones
for me, because I really struggled with sober
socializing of any type at the time, but I have
found that I have got a whole lot better at the
coffee and a muffin kind of visit over the years!
You can bake almost anything from cookies to
muffins, cupcakes, and tarts. Who knew that

spoiling someone else could add such value to your life!

- **Crochet/knit something.**

This sounds like a granny-like thing to do and in some ways it is, but wow, I loved this and I still do. I actually learned the art of arm-knitting. If you are looking to pass a bit of time, you should look up "blanket arm knitting" videos on YouTube. It is a brilliant way to pass the time, especially in the free evening hours. The result is a beautiful, thick blanket. If you have kids, they will love getting involved in this one too. I use thick synthetic wool and on an evening where I am feeling the urge to drink, because I am bored or "just because", I whip out my wool and I get knitting. I have also crocheted some slouch beanies, which other people have liked so much that I have sold them!

- **Try out an escape room.**

Trying out an escape room is something that I have always wanted to do, so naturally it ended up on my list. Unfortunately, I could never get my drinking buddies to down their glasses for one afternoon or evening, to do it with me. Most areas around the world have different versions of these rooms and they are heaps of fun. If you haven't discovered an escape room yet, the basic concept is for a team of players to work together to discover clues, solve puzzles, and finish tasks in a room in order to escape the room or achieve a specific goal. They can take several minutes to several hours to complete. If you haven't tried your hand at one of these yet, you *must!* I find them a worthy way to pass the time. We have completed several of them; some with just the two of us and others with a group of friends. It's really a lot of fun. Typically, drinking isn't allowed inside the room (score!).

- **Add *something* nutritious to your life.**

Most people think about getting sober and healthy and think they should quit all of their eating habits and recreate their entire diet immediately. This shouldn't be the case. The point of getting sober is to try to become the best version of you, but this takes time. You don't need to overhaul your diet unless you are eating particularly badly. Instead, focus on adding something nutritious to your diet every now and again. I have got into the habit of eating an apple and handful of unsalted nuts every few days. On many of the occasions where we go out for a meal, I opt for the veg or salad side dish instead of fries. I also believe that the soul needs nutrition, so I read a daily devotional every morning, before I start work.

- **Plan a sober holiday.**

A lot of people dread getting sober when there is a holiday planned. In fact, spans of people will put off their sobriety for after the holiday, but what's the point in that? There will surely be future holidays that come up; so it's best to bite the bullet and start preparing for awesome sober holidays as soon as you can. I felt the same at first, until I realized just how much more I get out of a holiday if I am clear, conscious, and feeling good.

The thought of a holiday sans booze was foreign to me, but I was still keen and excited to start planning for one. I picked a destination and then I spent weeks – actually months – planning it. I searched to the ends of Google for destination advice, I used Trip Advisor to learn about tours and trails and things to do and see. By the end of it, I had a holiday better planned than any of the previous holidays I had gone on. And guess what?! Because of all the forethought and planning, and because I was sober for the actual holiday (which was packed with fun activities), we had the best holiday of our lives. We had daily activities planned that deterred the lazy holiday drinking mode most get into. We ate at restaurants I had confirmed had alcohol-free wines and beers on offer. And we stayed in areas that weren't situated in party central (yup, our stay in the pub loft apartment days are behind us!). Of course there were those "a cocktail would make this better" moments, but it's important to learn to push through them, so I used our first holiday as a learning curve. One word of advice; if you get the urge to drink while on a sober holiday, try not to give the urge too much air time in your mind. Don't let it get a foothold in your mind. Oh, and of course, take some quit lit along with you – that's a must!

- **Offer to do something nice for a friend.**

I found this particular task really valuable to me. At first, I wasn't sure where to start. I knew I wanted to do something nice for a friend, but I wasn't sure what. About half-way through the day, I caught myself having a text conversation with a friend who was having a particularly rough week. She was struggling with the kids, was having issues with the hubby, and felt utterly overwhelmed by all the housework that seemed to be piling up around her. That early afternoon, I whipped up a meal for 4 people, packaged it and dropped it off at her house, so that she could have a night off from cooking.

On another occasion, I offered to babysit a friend's children, so that she and her hubby could go on a much-needed and long overdue kid-free date night. When you choose to do something nice for someone, remember that it is all about the other person. Give some thought to what would be really kind and helpful to someone else and set out to do it.

- **De-clutter the house.**

I wrote this particular task on my #project sober task list, because I was feeling quite irritated at the time with the state of my home. It seemed like there was just clutter everywhere. I started small-scale though. I didn't tackle the entire house at once. I believe that would have been too stressful for me. I started on my wardrobe. I worked shelf by shelf through each and every item in there. If the clothing item wasn't what I wanted anymore, it went on the charity pile and the clothes I wanted to keep were packed neatly back in the cupboard. If you have kids, even more fun awaits you! You can go through their wardrobes too!

If you feel like you have made progress, you can then tackle another area of the home. I started with my wardrobe and then moved onto the bathroom as we have a huge cabinet beneath the basin that seems to always get jam-packed with random items. I have also managed to de-clutter my kitchen twice during the past few years. Feeling bored and need something to do? Get decluttering. Grab a bin bag and start shoving all those unwanted trash items into it. You will be surprised at just how satisfying this can be! A less cluttered and tidier home makes for a clearer mind set – trust me!

- **Learn something new and don't give up on it.**

I put this particular item on my list, because I tend to get bored with life quite easily. I was really lucky when I selected this one, as learning something new is a task that can be drawn out over several weeks and months at a time. While Kev wasn't as into it as I was, many nights he would actually join in with my learning missions, which really made me happy. What did I learn? Well, I approached Kev and said I wanted us to do something together - to learning something new, for fun. I didn't even mention that it was part of trying to stay sober – I didn't want to label it a "sober activity". He said he would *sometimes* join me and other times not, depending on the actual new thing I wanted to learn. I made a list of new things we could learn languidly along the way and to my excitement, he agreed to some of them. Of course you can learn something new alone, there's really no right or wrong way to do this!

I have done these "learn something new" tasks several times and have been thoroughly enjoying them along the way. You can use it to pass time in the evenings, over weekends – whenever! Here's what I have done so far:

> Learn a new language.

I have dabbled in some French (which was terribly hard), Dutch, and Spanish lessons. This is not to say that I am fluent in any of them, but I know enough to bumble through basic conversations. We have plans to travel in the future and knowing the basics of some of these languages will help greatly. I didn't join expensive classes or anything. Instead, I used the DuoLingo app found in the App store which is free.

➢ Learn to play golf (and putt-putt).

This is something that I thought I would never learn. Before my dad completely submerged in his alcoholism, he actually used to go and spend Saturdays on the golf course with his buddies. For some reason, the mere fact that it was my dad's sport (not that he owned it or anything, but you know what I mean), meant that I didn't want to learn it. In fact, I developed an aversion to it and would make snarky comments about people who loved and participated in the sport. Kev and I live very close to a golf course, so I decided I should at least give it a try. This is one of those tasks that Kev agreed to join me in. Now a few months later (and after watching many YouTube videos on how it's done), we can sort of play the game. We certainly aren't going to be entering any tournaments together, but the golf course is beautiful and the time spent walking and playing together has proven valuable.

➢ Learn to play lawn bowls.

It really came as a surprise to me that I thoroughly enjoy lawn bowls. If you look up lawn bowls online you will notice that it's the game of old ducks the world over. Old ladies and their husbands head to the lawn bowls pitch and play a few rounds. I hear it's the chosen form of socializing in retirement homes. While learning how to play lawn bowls, we were fortunate enough to meet quite a lot of older folk playing the game. We connected with many of them and they taught us the ropes. Now that we secretly already know how to play lawn bowls, we plan to hustle other oldies when we reach our twilight years. They will have no idea that we are pros by then!

> Learn to cook something new.

You don't have to be a professional chef or even have an interest in cooking to do this one, but wouldn't you like to whip up some delicious cupcakes, make a sweet treat tart, or create a saucy stew you have never tried before? Now that you have the time to do it, you really should. When I decided to go sober, I also decided to focus on going more plant-based. This provided the perfect opportunity to book a cooking class, so I could learn about creating delicious plant-based dishes that are nutritional too. That being said, you don't have to spend money on a cooking class. Instead you can learn a new recipe at home, thanks to the wonders of the internet.

I often hunt down great recipes online and try them out. YouTube is a great place for step by step recipes. This became my Sunday thing. I would gobble a quick breakfast, go for a long walk with Kev, and then come and cook up a feast of starters, mains, and desert to be enjoyed over the next couple of hours! It took hours to complete (I love to get creative with food) and the kitchen was in a state at the end of it, but it was so much fun to turn on the music, whip up something delicious and then present it to Kev.

These are just *some* of the sober project tasks that I threw myself into. In fact, I threw myself into these things; heart and soul. Having these activities or #project sober tasks are what saved me! They saved me from myself. They saved me from the poor thinking that a life without alcohol is a life of boredom. More importantly, they helped me move on from alcohol. There will come a day where the cravings are less, the urges are more subtle and you don't sit and think about alcohol all day long. As the famous Lennon quote goes "Life is what happens to you while you're busy making other plans". It's safe to say that your life *will* change and by keeping busy, the time will sail by smoothly and happily. That's what it's all about, right?

THE BEGINNING OF *YOUR* STORY

The end of this book is only the beginning of *your* story. Living life sober is undeniably rewarding. It takes time and effort to get right and at many intervals along the way you will feel like throwing in the towel and giving up, but here's the thing; Alcohol is a thief and it *will* steal from you – don't let it.

It will rob you of your relationships with your kids and family, as it gets you urgently wanting quality moments to pass, just so you can sink the next glass of your chosen poison.

It will rob you of meaningful experiences in your relationships with a partner as hangovers cloud quality time days, the effects of alcohol eliminate sex drive and spark unkind arguments, and nights meant for deep conversations and cuddling end in drunken stumbling and passing out.

It will rob you of your youth, as it presents your body with premature aging and wrinkling.

It will rob you of your health as it promotes cancer growth, heart disease, high blood pressure, and anxiety within you.

Don't be a victim of theft. Make the choice for a better life, because no matter how hard it is, we all know this; if I can do it, so can you. And you *will*. Keep going – one day at a time.

In the pages to follow you will find some personal recommendations - I hope you enjoy them!

I created this book with an abundance of love for *you*. Please take the time to leave a review of this book – it would really mean the world to me.

Movies & Documentaries about Sobriety, Alcohol, and Recovery

- My Name is Bill W (1989)

- Clean & Sober (1988)

- Basketball Diaries (1995)

- Trainspotting (1996)

- Requiem for a Dream (2000)

- 28 Days (2000)

- Intervention (2005)

- Rain in My Heart (2006)

- From Addiction to Recovery (Russell Brand) (2012)

- The Anonymous People (2013)

- Drinking to Oblivion (2016)

- The Truth About Alcohol (2016)

- Risky Drinking (2016)

- Trainspotting 2 (2017)

- Drinkers Like Me (2018)

- Mom (series on CBS)

These are just *some* of the movies, documentaries and series I have watched. I think the list of media out there is fairly extensive. Don't be put off by the age of some of these movies. They can be difficult to watch (some of them) but have been a good eye-opener for me.

QUIT LIT BOOKS

Want to read your way through the long nights, tough moments, and just to keep yourself on the right path? I can personally recommend the following books – all of which I have bought on Amazon. Here they are, in no particular order (just the order they are sitting on my book shelf in front of me, as I type this!)

- We Are The Luckiest by Laura McKowen

- Smashing Sobriety by Carla Kingsley & Lila Ross

- Sobertude by Dirk Foster

- The Sober Diaries by Clare Pooley

- _The Unexpected Joy of Being Sober_ by Catherine Gray

- _Another Love_ by Amanda Prowse

- _A Happier Hour_ by Rebecca Weller

- _Alcohol Explained_ by William Porter

- _Quit Like a Woman_ by Holly Whitaker

- _Sober As F***_ by Sarah Ordo

- _Recovery_ by Russell Brand

- _Rewired_ by Erica Spiegelman

- _Alcohol Lied to Me_ by Craig Beck

- _Blackout_ by Sarah Hepola

- _The Sober Survival Guide_ by Simon Chapple

- _Sober Lush_ by Amanda Eyre Ward

- _This Naked Mind_ by Annie Grace

- _Girl Walks Out of a Bar_ by Lisa Smith

- _Stumbling Into Sobriety_ by Tracy Collins

- <u>Mrs D is Going Without</u> by Lotta Dann

If you can, get them all. All of these books had parts in them that resonated with me so hard that I had several ah-huh moments. Those moments are vital when trying to do life alcohol-free.

Printed in Great Britain
by Amazon

46384658R00173